GRACE IN THE BLOOD

From Pain to Purpose - God is Not Done With Me

NATTALEE MITCHELL WARREN

GRACE IN THE BLOOD. Copyright @ 2025. Nattalee Mitchell Warren. All rights reserved.

No part of this publication may be reproduced, stored in a retrieval system or transmitted in any form or by any means, electronic, mechanical, photocopying, recording or otherwise without the prior written permission of the author.

Published by:

Editor: Cleveland O. McLeish (Author C. Orville McLeish)

ISBN: 978-1-965635-51-3 (Paperback)

Scripture quotations marked "KJV" are taken from the Holy Bible, King James Version (Public Domain).

Scripture quotations marked (NIV) are taken from the Holy Bible, New International Version®, NIV®. Copyright © 1973, 1978, 1984 by Biblica, Inc.™ Used by permission of Zondervan. All rights reserved worldwide.

Scripture quotations marked (NLT) are taken from the Holy Bible, New Living Translation, copyright © 1996, 2004, 2007 by Tyndale House Foundation. Used by permission of Tyndale House Publishers, Inc., Carol Stream, Illinois 60188. All rights reserved.

Scripture quotations marked "NKJV" are taken from the New King James Version. Copyright © 1982 by Thomas Nelson, Inc. Used by permission. All rights reserved. Bible text from the New King James Version® is not to be reproduced in copies or otherwise by any means except as permitted in writing by Thomas Nelson, Inc., Attn: Bible Rights and Permissions, P.O. Box 141000, Nashville, TN 37214-1000.

Scripture quotations marked "ESV" are from the ESV Bible® (The Holy Bible, English Standard Version®), copyright © 2001 by Crossway Bibles, a publishing ministry of Good News Publishers. Used by permission. All rights reserved.

The Holy Bible, Berean Study Bible, BSB. Copyright ©2016, 2020 by Bible Hub. Used by Permission. All Rights Reserved Worldwide.

Dedication

To every sickle cell warrior—your strength is sacred, your story matters.

To my family, thank you for being my anchor through every storm.

To my pastor and church family, your prayers and love carried me when I couldn't carry myself.

To my Principal, Mr. George Goode, my community, coworkers, and donors—your compassion, support, and generosity were lifelines. Thank you for believing in me.

And to Jesus Christ, who gave me grace in the blood and purpose in my pain—You turned my suffering into a song, my weakness into worship, and my scars into a story worth telling.

This is for the battles I survived, and the glory that followed.

Acknowledgments

Upon the completion of this encounter, first and foremost, I owe an immeasurable debt of gratitude to my Lord and Savior, for His grace was truly in my blood, sustaining me through unimaginable pain and suffering. I give all glory and honour to Him. Writing "Grace in The Blood" was not just an act of sharing my story, but a profound testament to the transformative power of faith and community.

To my dear pastor, Doreen Williams, your fervent prayers and unwavering spiritual covering carried me through some of the darkest and most painful seasons. You spoke life when my strength was failing, and your obedience to God's voice helped guide me back to hope.

To my church family, House of Prayer COGOP, Church Pen, your love, intercession, encouragement, and spiritual support were a lifeline. You stood in the gap, lifted my hands, and never stopped believing with me.

To my immediate family, Agustus Warren, my husband of eighteen years, I honour you; my children Allayne Warren (Precious), Alwayne Warren (Promise) and my mentee Kayla Johnson, your presence, sacrifices, and unconditional love has been remarkable. Thank you for standing with me, weeping with me, and celebrating each moment of progress. Your support gave me the courage to press on when everything in me wanted to give up.

To my sister-in-law Shaneil Livingston-Walker, my siblings Roshell Walker-Speare, Gavin Austin and Crusezon Walker, thank you for being there for me every step of the way. Your support was immeasurable; I truly give God thanks for you.

To Evangelist Moveen Williams and the members of The God Prayer Line and to the many servants of God who released the continuous prophetic words over my life—you reminded me of God's promises when I had forgotten how to dream. Your words were a lifeline, tethering me to destiny when despair tried to sever all connection to purpose.

To the donors and supporters who gave out of love, compassion, and obedience—thank you for being a part of this miracle. Your generosity helped carry me when I had no strength left to carry myself.

Finally, to every sickle cell warrior reading this: your story matters. There is grace in your blood too. May you find healing, hope, and the courage to keep going.

This book is for all of us—for every tear, every prayer, every breakthrough. It is a witness to restoration.

With a grateful heart,
Nattalee Mitchell-Warren

Table of Contents

Dedication iii
Acknowledgments v
Chapter 1: Born For Battle 9
Chapter 2: Thursday's Miracle 17
Chapter 3: Cries In The Night, Whispers From Heaven ... 23
Chapter 4: Purpose in the Pain 31
Chapter 5: The Valley Of Decision 45
Chapter 6: Faith That Fights Back 49
Chapter 7: The Threshing 63
Chapter 8: When Pain Meets Prophecy 69
Chapter 9: Warfare And Wellness 91
Chapter 10: Miracles In The Mundane 95
Chapter 11: Rewriting The Narrative 103
References 109

Chapter 1

Born For Battle

"God is not done with me. He is just getting started, and I am right here for it!"

Approaching the age of forty, I had a lot of mixed emotions. I was happy because it is often said that life begins at forty; I believe this to be true. Additionally, my children were no longer as dependent, and I was experiencing a great level of emotional freedom. On the other hand, I was scared because I didn't know what the years ahead would bring, and I was thinking, *"Girl, you are getting old!"*

I have always believed in the prophetic word, but I have rarely received one. If I remember correctly, my first ever personal prophetic word was when my daughter was about eight years old, the same year she was baptized. It was meaningful and intense, but nothing compared to when I turned forty.

It all began a week before my birthday. I accidentally slipped at work and ended up with a minor fracture on my left ankle. I celebrated my birthday, nevertheless, in fine style with my church family, children, and friends. About a month after that, I started having pain in my right hip, buttocks, and lower back. As a part of routine screening, I went to the eye clinic and was told that I had glaucoma, but after doing scans, the results were inconclusive. I was sent to do an MRI, which revealed some demyelination in the brain. I was placed on a strict diet and was referred to a neurologist, but I could not get an appointment as available dates were several months ahead. All this time, I was still having hip pain, which began to get worse over time. Being a sickle cell warrior, pain was a regular thing, so I just thought it was the norm, and I took my painkillers. After days of no relief, I went to get an injection from my doctor. This did not help either, so I officially went to the doctor for a diagnosis. It was then that I was told it could be a pinched nerve, and I started treatment for that.

Days turned into weeks, and weeks turned into months. I decided to see a different doctor, who sent me for an X-ray, but the scan came back showing nothing, so I continued working. By this time, I had started limping because of the pain. This continued for several weeks as I focused on taking my students through PEP exams and working six days a week, teaching with every fiber of my being.

As a child of God, I am passionate about attending church, praying, fasting, and living a life dedicated to God. One

Sunday, I attended church, and my pastor was preaching. She called me up, laid hands on me, and said, *"The Lord said to declare over you, you shall not die but live and declare the works of the Lord."* She then told me I should declare it over my life every day, and I did, when I remembered. God also instructed me to partake of the Lord's Supper twice daily, which I did, morning and night, for several weeks, and this brought me great relief. However, consistency was a major problem I had. I stopped taking the Lord's Supper and had completely forgotten about it for a long time. I did not know what God was protecting me from and yet preparing me for.

By April, I was limping more; the pain was worse, and I had to take painkillers to cope. On April 23, 2023, a pastor from Trinidad visited my church to minister. She called me out and ministered in my ears, saying, *"Nattalee, you have poured out a lot and now you are drained, but God is releasing a new grace in you today. He is giving you a fresh anointing, and every attack on your health is canceled."* After her message, she came back to me personally and said, *"God is replenishing you. Everything you are going through with your health and otherwise, He is taking you through them. Be strong, be encouraged."*

This was at the end of the PEP exam season, and I was truly exhausted; however, the school year was not yet finished, and I had my two-year-old nephew to care for, along with my family. That grace was surely on time and very needed for that season.

A month later, a minister from the United States visited and ministered at our church. As she ministered that Sunday, she stopped to ask who was forty years old. I did not respond at first because I was surprised and was also looking to see if anyone else was forty. She asked again, and I reluctantly raised my hand as I discovered I was the only one in the congregation at that age. She called me to the altar and prophesied over my life, speaking several positive things. But to my astonishment, she ended by saying, *"Do not be afraid. No weapon formed against you shall prosper, and every tongue that rises against you is condemned; this is your heritage."* I cried and worshiped because it was just moments before, as the praise team led worship, that I had been talking to God in my heart, asking, *"God, are You really going to have me serving You like this?"* The pain and swelling in my foot were becoming unbearable. I was thinking, *"God, you blessed me with a new car, but the devil does not want me to drive it."* As time went by, I was in pain all day, every day. I had to take painkillers to get through each day. Sometimes, I push through with tears in my eyes. As a grade six teacher, a lot was expected of me, so I prayed and pushed through the pain. Sometimes the limping was so severe that I felt embarrassed just being seen and questioned by colleagues.

It was approaching the end of the school year, and I had a pattern: painkillers at night and extra painkillers for a long day.

I had booked a two-week vacation to Atlanta for August and was really looking forward to it. In my mind, I thought that if I could get enough rest, my foot would be okay for me to return to work in September. Through all of this, the prophetic words continued, but God did not stop speaking.

At the end of June, I went to a crusade with my worship team to lead worship. As the preacher preached, I went for a bathroom break. When I returned, the preacher called me out and said, *"God said to tell you that you were not born to face only the hardships, but also the good times. You shall not die! You have not preached your last message yet! Your season is about to change."* This could not have been more real. I felt like someone who was hypnotized. *What could this be?* I asked myself as the preacher's words penetrated my heart. Meanwhile, my current state looked insurmountable. I had to find the courage in me to hold on to the word as if it were life itself.

As the school year ended, I was also quite relieved that my sister came and relieved me of caring for my nephew. This was very satisfying. I was also dealing with other family issues, which drained me and made me flustered; I just couldn't wait for the month of August to begin since July also had a lot of work and stress of its own.

In July, I went for another follow-up appointment at the clinic where I did the scan. It turned out that the scan showed a diagnosis of stage three Avascular Necrosis; my hip bone had died due to a lack of blood and oxygen caused by sickle cell. It was concluded that I needed a hip replacement, and, to my surprise, the cost was approximately one million Jamaican dollars. I questioned the Lord, assuring Him that I knew He had a plan. I was aware of the need for the surgery to be done urgently, as I had to return to work.

I recall telling my pastor about the surgery, and she instantly became so uncomfortable to the point where she seemed upset. She was very uncomfortable about me needing surgery, and, if you know my pastor, she is going to pray about it. By this time, walking for me was very painful and very noticeable.

One afternoon, we had a funeral at church to bury one of our beloved sisters, and my pastor called a meeting with the members after the funeral, which was quite out of the norm. The main point of the meeting was that she was led to call the church to a three-day fast on behalf of those who were sick, especially on my behalf, because my case was urgent. At the time, I did not welcome the idea because I thought surgery would correct the situation. Little did I know that the devil had bigger plans, but when grace and favour locate you, it is something special. It was also very comforting that I had a Shepherd who watched for our souls and was steadfast about listening to God.

The plan of the enemy was to destroy my life, and he was quite cunning about it, but God had already gone before me and had declared, *"I will not die but live to declare the works of the Lord."* This was the reason my pastor's spirit would not be at peace regarding that surgery.

We started fasting, and after praying about it, I was fully on board. I really gave my all during the fast because I was determined that if God was doing and saying something, I would not be a hindrance. As the fast progressed, it became even more interesting. On the final night of the fast, while we were at church praying together, we got a call that a church sister had lost her daughter. I could not help but question the Lord in my heart as I wondered, *"God, what are you saying in all of this?'*

Some days after the fasting, about July 31st, I started feeling pain in my rib, which I first thought was gas pains. Then I associated it again with sickle cell crises, so I started to take painkillers. When it didn't stop, I visited my clinic on Tuesday to get a check-up. I was treated for the pain and released.

A few days later, the pain was back and more severe, so I returned to the clinic and was again treated and sent home. I was still in pain, but I thought it would get better. My ticket was booked for August 10 to visit the United States for two weeks. On Saturday, August 5, I woke up with severe chest pains along with the same rib pain I had before. Knowing the seriousness of chest pains, I decided to visit the Spanish Town hospital. My pastor was leaving for a trip to Barbados on the same day. When I told her of my pain and my intention to go to the hospital, she quickly came by my house, laid hands on me, and prayed a prayer of covering over me as she left. I was taken to the hospital by my brother and was sent to do a chest x-ray while they also took some blood. I was given painkillers and fluids and was later told that I had a chest infection, which was acute, and I would be admitted; however, there was no bed, so I spent the night on a chair. Because of the hip pain I was already having, the doctor tried all he could to get me a bed, but none was available. By the morning, my hip was very sore, my leg was swollen, and the chest pain was unbearable. Seeing that he was not able to help my situation, the doctor decided to send me home with medication. I was happy because a church dinner was coming up, and I didn't want to miss it!

Quite relieved and happy, I went home and stopped by church to see how preparations for the big day were going. There was a great celebration as everyone was glad to see me, thanks to the many prayers being said on my behalf. Of course, they ensured I headed straight home to rest. My church family is very caring, considerate, and hardworking.

To my great pleasure, I attended our annual church dinner, although I was warned and cautioned against overexertion. For the first time ever at this church, I left dinner early and went home. I was still not feeling my best, but I was on medication and preparing for my upcoming flight.

Chapter 2

Thursday's Miracle

Thursday, August 10, finally arrived. I was up at 3 am with my family, heading to Donald Sangster's International Airport for my 7 am flight. I was worried because I was feeling very sick; I had shortness of breath, and I did not know how I was going to manage flying with my already reduced oxygen level. I got there on time, said goodbye to my family, checked in, and was given a wheelchair because of my hip. A very nice attendant pushed me in the wheelchair to where we would start boarding and promised that she would return when it was time to board. While waiting, it was announced that all flights were cancelled due to trouble on the runway. I was given the option of staying over at an Airbnb and sharing the cost with another passenger, but something in me got very cross about the idea. I asked for a refund and headed straight to the Knutsford Express stop, where I booked a ride home. I was feeling relieved, but also disappointed. My sister-in-law, on the other hand, who was anticipating my arrival, was so disappointed that she fell asleep instantly with a terrible headache.

On my way back home, I started to rethink travelling again. I just could not be bothered. The summer was almost over, my two-week vacation was already cut short, and I just couldn't muster the courage and strength to deal with the stress amid all the sickness. I decided to call off the entire trip. Later, I discovered the miracle of that day. As children of the Most High God, it is essential for us to understand that delay does not mean denial and that nothing catches God by surprise. In every aspect and happening of our lives, He always has a plan. It is up to us to trust His plan. I pray that, like the disciples, we will consistently ask the Lord to increase our faith.

I got home, and my sister-in-law was up and on the phone, trying to rebook another flight despite my wishes. With my brother on her side, I had no choice but to let them do as they wished. I did not know that while my pastor was in Barbados, she called on the prayer team to pray that I would still go on this trip because she was convinced that something was wrong and my doctors were overlooking some key issues. She was convinced that if I traveled abroad, I would be able to see a doctor there, and they would find the root of the problem.

Later that evening, I was informed that my flight had been rebooked with another airline, and my brother would be my driver to the airport. Little did I know that this was a divine

GRACE IN THE BLOOD

setup. Saturday morning arrived, and my brother was there earlier than expected; I had to ask for extra time to get ready. Thankfully, I was feeling much better as my breathing had improved. My brother helped me finalize my packing while I tried to get ready as quickly as possible; after a short while, we were off. It was a long but relaxing ride to the airport; we had genuine communication along the way, and I used the opportunity to take a couple of snapshots. I always loved going on long rides with my siblings because we could talk about anything and feel relaxed, open, and honest. Saying goodbye to him that day was hard because it had been a while since we shared such a connection with each other. I missed him and wished we could go together. The flight was on time and very relaxing. Thanks to Wi-Fi, I was able to keep my family posted throughout the flight, which eased their nervousness. We arrived in Atlanta quite peacefully. Checking out was lengthy, but before long, I was in the car heading home with my sister-in-law, who was very excited and relieved that I had arrived safely. We talked on our way home and shared exciting stories and laughter. It was my first time travelling to Atlanta, Georgia, and I was genuinely happy.

The next morning, we went to the store to get food supplies. I grabbed my jacket, and my sister-in-law gave me a weird look as she asked, *"What are you going to do with that? It is hot here; it's summer."* Recapturing the many times I traveled to New Jersey and New York, I replied, *"Foreign always cold for me, even in summer."* She smiled and replied, *"Okay, if you think so."* We headed for the door, but as soon as I stepped outside, I exclaimed, *"Oh my gosh, I am in Jamaica!"* It was very hot. We laughed loudly as we walked towards the car.

As I started settling down in Atlanta, I started feeling sick again. By Tuesday, I was in a lot of pain, but I continued with the medication and fought it in silence. I recall Tuesday night; I was home alone, as my sister worked night shifts. I was in pain, but I lay down and ate an apple. After eating the apple, I started having a stomach ache along with all the chest and hip pain I was already having. I broke out in prayer and tears as I rolled on the floor. I screamed the words of Psalm 103:13, *"As a father shows compassion to his children, so the Lord shows compassion to those who fear him."* (ESV), and I challenged God, saying, *"God, You said You are a compassionate Father, and in all of this pain, You expect me to bear a stomach ache too? Lord, You said You would not give me more than I can bear, but this, Lord, is too much. I cannot bear anymore!"* I cried out on the floor as I writhed in pain. Moments later, the bellyache suddenly stopped. I returned to the bed and whispered, *"Thank You, Daddy."* He heard me. He answered, and just like that, I was off to sleep peacefully.

The next day, I was feeling a little better, but something was still obviously wrong; however, I kept pushing through. That night, I was alone again, but we had a church leader's meeting via Zoom. After the meeting, we opened our mics to say goodbye. As I spoke, one church sister proceeded to ask why I was speaking in that manner. I was in a lot of pain and taking short breaths. I could not even lie down. I told her I was not feeling well. By the time I said it, everyone on the platform began praying for me. As the prayers went up, I began to feel better, so I was able to sleep.

The following morning, my sister-in-law came from work to find me still in bed. She checked on me and asked how the pain was. I did not want to tell her how bad the pain was because I knew she was tired from working all night. She looked at me as if she could see straight through me and said, *"I am taking you to the emergency room."* I replied, *"No, man, it's okay. I'll be okay. Just go get some rest."* But she insisted, and later that afternoon, I was at the hospital.

A DIAGNOSIS, NOT DESTINY

At first, the diagnosis was the same as I explained the rib pain, when it started, the treatment I was on, how I recently travelled for vacation, and now the pain has returned. I was almost certain that it was just an infection that had not been fully cleared up. The doctor understood and requested some tests and some medications. As I was there being prepared for treatment, they took some blood, and not long after, they took some more blood. This confused me, but I stayed calm. Again, another doctor came by and said that she would be taking me for a CT scan. I figured it was just like a chest X-ray, but more advanced since I was in a first-world country. When I returned, a new nurse came to me; this time, it was a male. He explained that he would be taking over my care and asked if the doctor had spoken to me. I told him no, but

I was wondering what the problem could have been. I wasn't worried at all; my sister-in-law was still there, so we kept talking a little.

A short while after, a female doctor came to me, her face looking a bit unsure of herself. She asked for my name and then said she had some not-so-good news. We listened attentively as she explained. *"A d-dimer blood test was done, and while its normal range would be 0-500, yours was over 24,000, so we did a CT, which revealed that you have blood clots in the lower lobe of your lungs. As a result, you will be admitted, and we need to start treatment right away."* I asked her, *"Is it one in one lung?"* She replied, *"No, there are multiple clots in both lungs."* My sister-in-law's eyes popped wide open, but I whispered, *"Thank You, Jesus!"* As I lay there, I began to recall all the prophetic words I had received in the weeks leading up to this and how God continued to repeat, *"You shall not die."* It all started to make sense to me. *"Well, God already said I would not die, so I guess they will know what to do and I will get through this,"* I thought to myself, reassuringly.

When my pastor was updated, she began to cry while praising God, saying she knew something else was wrong, and she was overjoyed that I had taken the trip. Then she reassured me that I would be fine. As my siblings got the call, they cried mercilessly. I had to take the phone and assure them that I was okay and that I needed them to give thanks to God for what He was doing and to pray for me now.

Chapter 3

Cries In The Night, Whispers From Heaven

While in the hospital, I was on IV blood thinner, fluids, oral and IV pain killers, IV antibiotics, oxygen, plus I had a heart monitoring device attached to me. Someone came every six hours to take some blood for testing. To make matters worse, ever so often, my veins would get so swollen that the IV would blow and they had to relocate them, sticking me all the time. I could barely talk. I was coughing all the time and was very weak. Although my hip was still bothering me, it became the least of my problems. I was so sick that even though my phone was right beside me, I could not reach over to pick it up. I could not feed myself a drink of water. In all of this, I was coping and holding on to the Word of God.

I remember vividly the Saturday night while in the hospital; I started to feel even worse. My oxygen level dropped, my blood pressure rose, my heart rate and temperature increased, and everything was going wrong. Nurses, Nurse

Technicians, and Doctors came in to run tests. A chest x-ray was done on the spot, an echocardiogram was done on the spot, and blood was taken for further tests. While all this was going on, I could only focus my heart on God as I spoke to Him, *"God, You gave me Your Word several times before I got here. You took me on a plane ride with clots in my body and caused me to make it here. You are not a man that You should lie. You said I will not die, so I know, God, that You are taking me through this."* I knew He heard me, and I could hear His divine whisper saying, *"Look up, child. I am right here with you."* After some time, I stabilized again. If you ever get to a place where only your mind and soul can speak to God, rest assured that He hears and His presence will locate you.

FROM PATIENT TO PREACHER

During my time in the hospital, I continued to take the Lord's Supper as often as possible. One day, my wine went bad; I had to throw it out and wait for my sister-in-law to bring me a new one. As I was there, the chaplain of the hospital paid me a visit. He wanted to know how I was doing mentally and spiritually, and if there was anything he could do to enhance my spiritual connection with my God. I told him I was happy despite the circumstances because I knew God had a plan in all of this, and that I could see God's hand in my situation, though it may seem uncertain. I assured him that it was by God's grace that I was still there, and I am trusting God in my process. He stood there for a long while as he seemed dumbfounded by my response, as if he was allowing it all to soak in. After a moment of silence, he finally spoke, saying, *"Wow!"* He asked if there was anything I needed, and I told him, *"Yes, I could do well with some communion packs."* He agreed and went to get them; we had communion together.

After that visit, he would come at other times to check on me as usual. We would then have the Lord's body and blood together and pray. Afterward, I learned that chaplains would normally visit patients whom they thought would not survive to offer them some solace during their transition. But thanks be to Jehovah God, who holds the keys to my life. I was used to minister hope to him instead of receiving the 'solace' he was meant to bring me.

One day, while still in the hospital, my sister-in-law called me, and she was very sad. She had to do some tests and medical checks for a new job that she was seeking. During the process, she was told that they had identified a legion, and she needed to do further testing. This left her distraught. I told her to come and see me right away.

As she came into my hospital room, I motioned for her to come onto my bed beside me. I hugged her, and I rebuked the devourer in the name of Jesus. I was reminded of Hebrews 6:10, *"For God is not unjust. He will not forget your work and the labor of love you have shown for His name as you have ministered to the saints and continue to do so." (BSB)*. With that, I began to declare that the devil would not have a hold on her, not after all God has allowed her to do for me. I prayed for her, declaring the Word, and then assured her to go and take the test they required because it would be well. Days later, she received her results and it was indeed well.

After nine days, I was released from the hospital with guidelines to not travel for two weeks, medication, and instructions on how to get further check-ups in a few days. By this time, I had to make arrangements to take some time off from work, as I was expected to return in September; however, that was no longer possible. My principal was very understanding and assured me that everything would be fine. I was on my way to recovery, but I had a long way to go. However, every step of the way, I could see the hand of God working out everything for my good.

As I remained in Atlanta, I started to make the most of my time there. After all, I was meant to be on vacation. My birthday was soon approaching, and I wanted to spend it there. I felt at peace as I reflected on how many people I knew who died just before their birthdays and how merciful God was to me. Meanwhile, my pastor and sister insisted that I not travel alone; arrangements were made for my best friend, my sister from another mother, to come to Atlanta to take me home. I am so blessed! My sister-in-law also had a surprise up her sleeve. She prepared to bake my birthday cake and set up decorations for my birthday. She also took me out for dinner and bought me a teddy bear that sang *"Happy Birthday."* I will never forget it.

My best friend came, and we had a very good time together. It was like three sisters living in the same house, and they made my birthday extra special.

GRACE IN EVERY CRISIS

The day to return home was approaching, and for some reason, I was feeling quite fearful. I feared travelling, even though I was still on blood thinners. I prayed, but I still felt fear. The Sunday after my birthday, we decided to attend church, as I was heading home that same week. We were undecided on which church to attend, and the three of us discussed it. My sister-in-law wanted us to visit her friend's church, but my friend and I found a church on Google that was affiliated with our church back home. I prayed about it, and in the end, we all decided on the church from Google, which was only seven minutes away. That morning, we got dressed and headed out. To our surprise, upon arrival, we found a church with very few black people. We were on time for worship and the Word. God was intentional about speaking to me that Sunday.

As the pastor began his message, he used the text from Isaiah 46, and his theme was, *"God said I have made you, and I will carry you."* All the fear I was feeling and the assuring words of God were suddenly erasing the many negative thoughts that were going through my mind through His servant. The exhortation that even to my gray hairs, my God would carry me and that He already knew the end of my story from the very beginning was simply amazing. I could not hold back the tears as I embraced the words falling from his mouth, which came straight from the Bible. It was as if that scripture was written just for me, and God was just speaking directly to me in that moment. It was the first time I could remember hearing or reading that scripture. It was such a blessing. I went home in awe, *"How could God be so intentional?"* I thought.

Feeling much more confident, I began to pack for home. I learned that every now and then, we as children of God need to be reassured of who we are and whose we are. We are never too holy or righteous to become vulnerable. Being reassured by the Word of God brought great peace to me, and I was no longer fearful; I was ready to take to the skies.

Our flight was a long and tiring one, with a four-hour layover that was also delayed, so it lasted all day. Even though we left at 3 a.m. that morning, we did not arrive in Jamaica until about 7 p.m. that evening. I was exhausted, but I was happy to be home to surprise my kids. Through all this, God was faithful because He had carried us. Grace was my portion.

After settling in at home and taking a few days to rest, I made some medical appointments to get my health sorted out, as I still had pain in my hip, and I was now walking with a cane. In addition, my left shoulder was in so much pain that I could hardly use my hand. I went to my family doctor to get an urgent prescription for blood thinners, which was running low, and I was instructed to take them continuously for three months without stopping. I told my doctor about the excruciating pains I had in my left shoulder and told him I needed to do a scan on it. He gave me the request. I did an X-ray, which concluded that there was Avascular Necrosis in my left shoulder as well. My doctor was dumbfounded, as he had hoped it wasn't that. He consistently apologized and said he was truly sorry that I had to go through all of this, and advised me to take the scan to my next orthopedic appointment. Despite all I was going through, I felt thankful, especially after the ordeal I had previously endured. For some reason, I was assured that it is well.

A few days later, I visited the sickle cell clinic, where I updated them on my latest health episodes. They convinced me to start a medication called Hydroxyurea to improve my blood count number and sizes, and to prevent further Avascular Necrosis AVN of the joints. I had been praying about this and felt the peace I usually seek before making a decision, so I was ready. I was told to undergo blood tests and other prerequisites, and I looked forward to it with much hope. I continued to attend my regular appointments with both the orthopedic clinic and the sickle cell unit. The surgery date was scheduled for December 13, 2023, and I was placed on a new medication to improve my red blood cell count.

In July, when I was initially diagnosed with the hip condition, I was told that in order to do the operation, I needed to buy a replacement hip and pay the surgical fees to the hospital before a surgery date could be set. My next appointment would have been August 10, the same day as my flight. I went back to the clerk and asked if I could be given a different date, and I was told that was the only one available because all other dates were full. I sighed, and my brother asked, *"What will you do?"* I told him, *"I will see what God is up to."* I was not going to miss my flight.

After checking the cost of surgery and the implant, I realized that I needed just a little under a million dollars; my health insurance would cover my hospital fees, but I would have to purchase the implant and then claim it afterward. The cost of the implant was six hundred thousand Jamaican dollars. I was very surprised by the cost, and I knew I didn't have that kind of money, but I trusted God that He had a way out. I was informed that I could apply for financial assistance through the Social Work Office at the hospital, which the Ministry of Health funds. I completed this and submitted all the required documents promptly to ensure the request was processed.

Chapter 4

Purpose in the Pain

Since I did not keep my August 10 appointment, and I did not return to Jamaica until the third week in September, I was given another Orthopedic appointment for October. By that time, I had gone through the pulmonary embolism and was placed on blood thinners for three months, which would end in November. I was not able to do surgery before that. During that waiting period, I was at home scrolling through the internet and came upon an article about stem cell therapy as an alternative method for treating Avascular Necrosis. To my delight, I jumped on the article and started reading. At the end, it presented a form to be completed for more information. I completed the form and, in a few hours, I received a call that gave me a wealth of information. However, I was disappointed to learn that the treatment was offered in India, and I thought that was a stretch. Nevertheless, it was only a matter of developing my trust in God.

That experience taught me how to pray and believe for what I wanted much more than before. When I went to the clinic in October, I was upgraded to two cases of AVN instead of one and was told that I could not be placed on the list for implant surgery until I had the receipt for the six hundred thousand dollars. I was taken aback. I was now approaching my maximum paid sick days, so I needed the surgery scheduled so I could figure out how to apply for additional time off from work. All of this was the enemy's plan to frustrate me. I was honestly anxious about getting through all of this, and I was nervous about my job. No wonder Philippians reminds us to be anxious for nothing, but to pray over everything so we can experience the peace of God (see Philippians 4:6). God's timing is paramount for all our situations; nothing catches Him by surprise. The problem is our lack of trust in God. I was learning some very valuable life lessons for my continued Christian journey.

My shoulder X-ray CD was stuck in the doctor's CD player and would not come out, so I was given another appointment to return in two weeks for a shoulder MRI before my next clinic date. Right after my appointment, I went to the social worker's office to check up on the status of my request. To my surprise, they had not made any progress since July. It was as if I never applied. I went back three other times; the result was the same. No one could explain to me what was happening, except for the secretary mumbling under her breath that the government had no money.

I went home and prayed. I asked God to awaken the soul of that social worker and cause my documents to be identified. I also prayed that God would grant me favour with the right surgery date, even though I still had no idea how I would source the money for the implant.

The following week, I underwent an MRI and returned for my appointment. The doctor I saw this time was very patient and kind. He reviewed my case carefully and then called another doctor to also review my MRI results. As they had their medical discussion, I sat there and nodded in agreement to what they were proposing. It was evident that my case was a rare one as they had a team for upper body surgeries and a different team for lower body; I had both. As an answer to my prayer, he went on his system and booked me into a space that already had a name slated for the date; beside my name, he wrote '*priority.*' I left that day feeling a lot more hopeful. I talked to God. *"Lord, I know You're not big on details, so please help me to follow You and obey each step of the way,"* I whispered.

On October 28, I attended a prayer breakfast at my church. As I sat in the congregation and listened to the guest speaker, it was as if she was speaking directly to me. The message was so encouraging, and the highlight for me was when she mentioned how Paul asked God to remove the thorn from his flesh, but the Lord replied, *"My grace is sufficient"* (see 2 Corinthians 12:9).

"Regardless of what you may be going through, give credit to God; all you need is grace. God is in the good and the bad, but He has provided us with grace." As the words left her mouth, they soothed my heart like medicine.

After her message, she called me up to pray for me, and she said to me, *"God will finish what He started. You are going to have a testimony. I see your cells warring against each other, but God is healing you, and He will give you a testimony."* This lady knew absolutely nothing about me to know I was suffering from sickle cell disease, but, yet another time, my God spoke.

I was home that week when the Holy Spirit told me to reach out to someone else to ask for financial assistance. I obeyed, and the first impression was not good; however, knowing the Lord had directed me, I held my peace and pursued my request. I was now being treated a little nicer. I was instructed to write a letter and hand it to him, and he would then forward it to the source from which I could access the assistance I was seeking.

In about two weeks, my mind kept urging me to call the person to follow up on the request. I now know that it was the Holy Spirit, but I had kept dismissing the thought, still a little disappointed about the person's attitude and having promised myself that I would not interact with him again. By the end of the following week, I woke up one Friday morning and heard the Holy Spirit speak to me clearly, saying, *"Make that call right now."* I felt a sense of peace, so I picked up the phone and made the call. It was so pleasant. I unexpectedly got to speak to the person right away, and to my surprise, he said he was waiting for me to call, as they had lost my contact information and were hoping I would call back. I was asked to submit my contact information by the following Monday. By noon on Monday, I got a call requesting additional information. I was glad I responded to the voice of the Lord when He spoke: I could have missed my divine appointment if I had not.

In November 2023, my aunt introduced me to a prayer line via WhatsApp. On this line, there were people from several parts of the world, but it seemed some were possible family members. They met three days per week around midday and prayed until later in the afternoon. When I joined this group, I was very skeptical until I heard the Lord speak to me about this prayer line; I then began to commit myself to it, and the encounters began.

As the days went by, I decided to put on a cake sale to assist in earning some money that I knew would be needed for my recovery and treatment. I kept asking God to heal me instead of allowing me to go through the process of surgery. Honestly, I was afraid of the surgery, and I would prefer not to go through the process; however, this was something I did not tell anyone. While I was going through this, I recall being on the prayer line, which was new to me, and prayers were being made for me. A lady I was sure knew nothing about me spoke to me using this song, *"Tis so sweet to trust in Jesus."* She recited all the verses of the song and went on to say, *"God wants you to continue to trust Him. He has chosen the process to heal you, and it will be alright."*

As the weeks went by, I was nearing the date to the end of taking the blood thinners and approaching the surgery date, but I still did not have the money to purchase the needed implant for the surgery that I would need to present one week before the surgery date.

There is something about going through the crushing times of your life. You can either go through it resenting the process, trying to shorten it, questioning God, or waiting it out, trusting and knowing that God is in control. I believe I chose the latter, even though there were days I cried and bawled to God when I screeched in pain. Crushing is not an easy process.

One of the deepest revelations God gave me in this process was that the word "trust" means *"I do not know or understand."* If we knew the outcome and understood the process from the beginning, then what would be the use of trusting? It is in looking back that you understand and see God's hand in your crushing, and that is the main reason we have to trust Him at the start.

During my crushing, I came upon the song entitled "The Story I'll Tell." It became my favourite song, and I would worship and cry every time I sang or listened to it, because my current situation was reflected in that song, and I was convinced I would have a story to tell in the future. I also came to realize that in every season of my life, God always gave me a song for that season; this was my song for that particular time.

It was November 14, 2023, and I was still waiting on the funds to purchase the implant for the surgery; however, I was open to whatever God would allow to happen for me SUDDENLY.

On Tuesday, November 28, 2023, I had an exciting and fulfilling experience. My daughter had her first CSEC practical exam, and though I could barely walk, I was very invested in it. I set out very early, along with my brother and best friend, to take her to school and help her set up her balloon arrangement. Of course, I was more of an emotional help than a physical one, but I had to be there. We must take a moment to thank God for the beautiful people in our lives and appreciate them. My friend took time off from work, and my brother made himself available to be there to support and encourage the process.

It was a spectacular day. She made us very proud by scoring full marks on her practical. After the practical, I visited an organization where I had previously applied for financial assistance for my surgery. I made the application in July and did not get a response. In October, I had the opportunity to reapply and was told they would be meeting on the last Thursday in November, which was the previous week. I was going there with the intention that my application would be approved, especially since I was two weeks away from my surgery date and one week away from my pre-op date. When I arrived, to my surprise, the secretary went through about 200 approved applications, but there was none for me. She proceeded to send me over to the HR department. When I arrived, I spoke to the person in charge, and God would have it that she went ahead and approved my application. My letter was completed right on the spot in under twenty minutes. Look at the favor of God! That same day, I was able to bring my letter to the implant provider to reserve my implant for the specific date.

Just two days before my pre-op date. I had a visit at home from my principal, vice principal, guidance counsellor, and my grade coordinator. The team visited, and it was a pleasant experience; I was also fortunate to receive some much-needed funds towards the procedure. I believe all of this was God showing me that He had me, and I didn't need to worry. Sometimes we go through dark times, but God will always provide flickers of light along the way to give us hope. We just need to pay attention.

On the 7th of December 2023, I went back for my clinic appointment. The doctor reviewed my case and, to my surprise, he rescheduled my surgery. He said I needed to do several tests before surgery, and I needed to be approved for surgery by an anesthesiologist who would have to give me an appointment sometime later. I wondered if this was the first time they had seen a case like mine and why they had not followed this protocol before that day, especially since I had been waiting for so long. To make matters even worse,

I was hoping both surgeries would be done and my hip and shoulder would be addressed at the same time.

I was previously told that I would do some decompression on my shoulder, and my understanding was that that was a simple procedure to bring me some relief from the pain and would, by God's abundant healing grace, bring complete healing to that shoulder, preventing a total shoulder replacement. However, news flash: I needed two joint replacements. They would do the hip first, then I would recover and go back to do the shoulder. I was very disappointed, frustrated, scared, and hurt.

After scheduling the dates for the tests, I left feeling rather upset. As I sat in the car and thought about this whole ordeal, I said, *"God, I know this did not catch You by surprise, so You must have a plan. I wish I knew what the plan was, but I know You must have one, so what are You really saying in all of this?"* I did not get a response at the time, but I suddenly felt the urge to call my pastor, which I did. I explained to her that the surgery was pushed back, and I was just tired of the pain and wanted to get it over with. As I knew she would, she assured me that God had a plan, and I was to relax and pray because He definitely had a purpose for postponing the surgery. Little did I know that the purpose would soon be exposed.

That night, I prayed, asking God to reveal His purpose and let me know His divine will. The following day, on December 8, 2023, I was home alone, weeping to the Lord.

As I thought about doing two surgeries to insert two implants in my body with no guarantee to bring healing but merely some temporary relief from the current pain, I wept bitterly as I exclaimed, *"God! There must be another way. This cannot be it. God, I have heard how You heal the blind, the sick, and raise the dead, but I want to feel it and see it for myself. I want to experience this in my own body. God, You must have a way out of this. There is no way I am going through with these two surgeries."* Later that same day, I received a WhatsApp text from an organization called Medico Experts with an invitation to a webinar the following week, titled "Effective Non-Surgical Treatment for Avascular Necrosis." I was like, *"Oh, please, what is this?"* It required registering, and I thought to myself, *"There's no harm in listening, and it's free, so I will go ahead and register. Just in case I am up to it, I will listen in."*

A few days later, I recall being at home and going online in an effort to research something when I came across an ad for stem cell therapy in Montego Bay. I was taken aback because, as far as I knew, this treatment was not available in Jamaica. However, I clicked on it. I later found out that it was not offered in Jamaica, but that led me to come into contact with a patient care manager for an organization in Mexico that offered stem cell treatment. From our first conversation, I was convinced that God was speaking to me. I felt positive about our conversations. I went ahead and scheduled a one-on-one consultation with the doctor, which was pretty smooth and informative. My spirit was now leaning towards getting this treatment and not the surgery, but I still had some questions.

I realized that in September, I had made contact with a doctor from India who was also introducing me to stem cell therapy as a treatment for my condition. I was initially considering it, but the lack of proper communication caused me to lose interest, and I soon forgot about that and was focused on doing surgery. With the renewed interest in this kind of therapy, I decided to send a message to my previous patient care manager from India to say 'hello.' The first thing he asked was how my surgery went. I told him I did not do it, and he was happy, saying it could be a good thing for me, and it was not a coincidence, so I should attend the webinar on the weekend to get more information on alternative treatment, because he would much rather I avoid the surgery. It was at that point that I realized the previous WhatsApp message had come from the hospital where he worked, and he had me on his mind. I could not help but feel a warm embrace as I thought to myself, *"God, You must be saying something in all of this."*

Saturday, December 16, came, and at 5 am, my phone rang, waking me from my sleep. It was the care manager from India reminding me that the meeting was about to start. I had asked my sister and sister-in-law to join me on the webinar for clarity and support, so I reached out to them, and they both joined as well. The webinar was very informative and interesting, as it also offered discounts on prices for those who attended at the time and would require the treatment.

My sister was eligible for one of the highest discount packages; she did not hesitate to interact, ensuring she secured one on my behalf. Although this was intriguing, I still had some reservations as I knew my case was somewhat unique and needed a treatment plan tailored specifically for me.

After the webinar, we were advised to book a one-on-one consultation with the doctor. This doctor was the head of orthopedics at his hospital in India, with over 32 years of experience in the field and over 18 years of experience treating avascular necrosis using stem cell therapy. I felt honored to have consulted with him one-on-one.

I explained my case to him, and he requested that I do some additional scans to send to him before he could come up with a definite treatment plan for me. I must say I admired his honesty. He sounded quite aware of what he was dealing with. I had a good session with him, and he answered all the questions my sisters and I had.

At the end of the session, I lay in bed thinking. Although I knew my case was unique and required much more patience and attention, I began to think about the cost, the distance I would have to travel, and all the difficulties. At that specific moment, all I could see were the impossibilities—all the reasons why this would never happen. But in that moment, God would have it that the patient care manager sent me a text encouraging me to do all I could to get the tests done and to ensure I get the treatment instead of the surgery. I replied, telling him I wanted to, but it just seemed so expensive and far-fetched. To my surprise, this was his reply: *"Have faith and God will make a way. He made you meet us. Last time we spoke, you were on the verge of getting the surgery, but again, you got the link and joined the webinar, and things are starting good again, thanks to the Almighty!"* I was at a loss for words as God used this indian doctor to realign my perspective. I agreed with him, and I was back on track.

Starting out with stem cell therapy on my mind in September, getting the hip transplant completely paid for, having the surgery rescheduled, then coming back to stem cell therapy with connections in Mexico and India, I had no doubt that God was definitely saying something at this point. I only needed to pray through this to gain complete clarity. I was led to have a sit-down with my pastor to explain all the happenings to her, which I did. The perspective was the same. God had given us a mandate of three days of fasting each month from my situation started, and He said we should continue. The three days of fasting continued, and we prayed for divine direction, trusting that God would reveal His complete will.

As I am writing this section, I am reminded of the word in Philippians 4:6-7: *"Do not be anxious about anything, but in every situation, by prayer and petition, with thanksgiving, present your requests to God. And the peace of God, which transcends all understanding, will guard your hearts and your minds in Christ Jesus." (NIV)*. With this in mind, I was off to pray and rest sweetly.

Chapter 5

The Valley Of Decision

As we approached the Christmas season, I had a virtual consultation with the orthopedic specialist from India. During this consultation, he explained that in order to have a full understanding of my condition and to make a proper diagnosis, he needed me to do additional tests, especially because my right foot was shorter than the left and I was having more pain. I agreed. It turned out that the AVN, which was at stage three, had now progressed to stage four and seemed to be affecting my knee as well. It was sufficient to say that my condition was getting worse and at a rapid rate. I was now very concerned about my other joints and bones.

After the specialist reviewed the tests, another consultation was arranged to discuss the line of treatment. At that point, he explained that due to the deteriorating condition of the hip joint, it was certain that a hip replacement was mandatory, as stem cells would not restore a femur that had collapsed and also correct the limb shortening. He further stated that stem cell therapy would be very useful in helping the shoulder and knee joints heal and prevent the progression of the condition to other joints and bones. The doctor also recommended that if I do the hip replacement surgery along with the stem cell therapy at the same time, it would add more value to the healing of the condition and speed up the healing of the surgery. It sounded like a plan, but I was waiting for the total cost of the treatment to determine my next steps. Performing the surgery in Jamaica would be cheaper, as I would not have to pay for the implant, and my insurance would cover approximately ninety percent of the hospital costs. However, this would mean waiting until I recover from the surgery to get the stem cell therapy, which would take me at least to summer since I would have to return to work as soon as I was healed from surgery. This would mean time in between and could cause more progression to other bones and a worsening of the condition in my shoulder and knees. I was in the valley of decision, and the only result was to turn to God and trust God.

I started to see the reason the surgery was postponed. God wanted me to consider this alternative. I knew God was saying something, but I was still not a hundred percent sure what it was. Yet again, I was reminded that trust means you do not see the way out, and your mind is limited, but you are confident that God has a plan. I know God is not big on details. He requires patience, obedience, and total confidence in Him, so I was learning to rest in Him daily.

The Christmas holiday started, and I was determined to make the most of it. We had a day of fellowship at church, family dinner and games at home, and I rested. On December 27th, I had some tests scheduled with my UWHI doctors, and since I was unsure of my final decision, I went ahead and had the tests done. I also wanted to check the results to see if I was fit enough for traveling to India. I had received the treatment cost in India and discovered that it was approximately one and a half million dollars to cover the total treatment, inclusive of the hip replacement surgery and the implant. This would also require an additional $500,000 to cover flights, as I needed at least one person to travel with me, and India is very far from Jamaica.

Chapter 6

Faith That Fights Back

I decided to return to the organization that had committed to paying for the hip implant for the surgery to be performed at UHWI. I had expected that they would be able to transfer the funds to my new line of treatment and possibly add some additional funds for my treatment. When I arrived, I realized that a fund for treatment abroad was actually available, but a different department within the organization managed it, and I needed to apply separately to that department. Additionally, I needed two different medical reports from local hospital doctors to confirm that I had the condition and that treatment was not available locally. This encouraged me a little as I thought all I needed was to get those letters.

I was able to get the proposed letter of the treatment cost printed at the same office, so I went to a health insurance office to submit it for approval. I was told they would not cover the procedure, but I could pay out of pocket and come back to claim. The agent further told me that several of their clients were Indians and would go back home to carry out several medical procedures, then return to claim. This got me rather excited, as I was thinking that even if I were to take a loan, I could always come back to claim and repay it. With these expectations, my heart was at ease, and since we were now heading into the holiday, I could rest peacefully.

The holidays went by swiftly. It was a remarkable time, especially celebrating the last day of the year as a Sunday, a family day, and Watch Night; it was uniquely awesome. January came, and the holidays were over; it was now down to crunch time, and I was given January 10th as a surgery date. I needed to decide whether to undergo surgery at UHWI or receive stem cell treatment in India. I had less than a quarter of the total funds I needed for India. It looked bleak.

I went to the sickle cell unit with the hope of getting the medical reports and dropping them off the same day. To my disappointment, I waited all day just to get one of the letters. I needed to go to my pre-op medical appointment at UHWI to apply for the second letter. To make matters worse, as I lay in bed the morning of January 3, 2024, I received a call. It was from the agent at the health insurance office, and she stated that, despite it being a new year, she had some not-so-good news. I calmly responded, "Okay," and she proceeded to inform me that after reviewing my letter, the company had instructed her to tell me that they would not cover any part of the treatment because they do not cover stem cell therapy, so I would have nothing to claim. I sighed and calmly ended the conversation. The Holy Spirit said, *"Pray."* I started talking to God, and when I was finished, the Spirit of God spoke these words to my heart, *"They will not cover it, but I will, and they only cover 80% but I cover one hundred percent (100%)."* I smiled broadly and replied, *"Yes, God."* That evening, I placed my hand on my **prayer wall** as a covenant with my God, and I said, *"Lord, tomorrow as I go to UHWI, let me meet the right doctor. Grant me favour with men and whatever You say tomorrow, Lord, it is final."*

It was January 4, and I left a little earlier than usual to make my appointment. I will never forget the part of my devotion that morning that stood out the most to me. I was reading the book "Because of Jesus, Today is Your Best Day," written by Roy Lessin. That morning, the title of the page I read said, *"Today is your best day because of God's presence."* The story reiterates that God gives the best because He is the best. God gives the best kind of peace, love, and joy. One specific line reads, *"His perfect love can only desire what is the highest, the greatest, and the absolute best for your life."* Right there and then, I could sense that that word was for me.

I waited patiently for my turn to see the doctor, but I was a little nervous as to what I would say to the doctor. *Would I propose that I was interested in another line of treatment and would not necessarily come back to do the surgery there?* My name was called and I went inside. First, I realized that all the doctors present were new and were not the ones I had seen in my previous appointments. The second thing I noticed was that they were fairly young too. By the time I could present my case, one doctor asked me one question and then told me he would have to reschedule my appointment, which also meant that my surgery would also be rescheduled. This was confirmation again that God was definitely saying something.

It is essential to note that, because God is in the story, it does not mean the enemy will not appear. He definitely will, and it will be in ways that really tempt you to question yourself about what God has said to you. I proceeded to introduce my case of treatment to him, and he straight up told me he did not think stem cell therapy works, and it would be better if I did it with a local doctor. I asked him for the letter to present my case to the Chief Medical Officer at the financial institution where I was requesting financial assistance. He was very unwilling to recommend it, but then told me I should ask at the front desk, and it would take up to two weeks to be ready. My surgery was rescheduled again because I needed to see the anesthesiologist first, and that appointment was due for the 9th. Now I had another appointment to return to the orthopedic clinic on the 11th. I responded to him in a gentle and willing manner, collecting all instructions before calmly walking away.

The morning of the 9th came, and I woke up very early to set out for Kingston. I remember talking to God before heading into the shower, then getting dressed. I did not feel like I was finished talking to God. I felt like I wanted to shout and scream out to Him. However, it was very early, and everyone would still be sleeping, and I did not want to disturb my family. I decided to rest my head and hands on my prayer wall, and I spoke to God with tears running down my cheeks. I was in anguish. I was in physical and emotional pain, which I could barely distinguish. One thing I reassured Him of was that I would keep trusting Him, but it was time He showed up.

I was following whatever lead God was taking. I did not know if the solution was India or UWHI; I just knew God had to do something. I was at risk of being brought to the medical board and losing my job; the health insurance office would not cover my procedure if I pursued it overseas, and I did not get the medical report from UWHI to take to the chief medical officer so I could pursue my application for financial assistance to pursue my treatment overseas. I still did not get a date for my surgery from ortho and, to make it all worse, I was not cleared by anesthesia, which made it impossible for the surgery to be scheduled. It literally seemed like I was nowhere, and I didn't know what to do. I was out of options and out of plans.

When I got home that evening, I had to let it out to God. I told Him He had to show up now. I needed answers. I told Him that for the sake of my faith, He had to show up. I needed a "now miracle," not tomorrow but NOW! *"I am tired, and You promise not to give me more than I can bear. Are You sure I can bear all of this? I do not think so, God. I am tired. You have to answer me NOW! You told me to wait,* and I did. You said trust You and I did. Answer me now, GOD!" I repeatedly cried.

I saw my son standing over the kitchen sink, and he held his head down over the sink while my daughter was locked in her room and came out later with swollen eyes; I knew she was crying. When I was finished, my son looked at me and said, *"Don't worry, Mommy. This will soon be over."* With the sweetest and most assuring smile I could muster, I looked at him and replied, *"Yes, my baby, this will soon be over, in Jesus' name,"* and I started to give God thanks for giving us strength to go through this and for choosing us to go through this test. I asked Him, *"God, please do not let us fail."*

ENCOUNTERS IN THE FIRE

That very night, after emptying my heart, I felt much better, so I went to take a shower and decided to continue writing my story while listening to some faith-building songs. My phone rang, and it was a call from one of the agents from the health insurance office. At first, I thought he was calling the wrong number, but then it became clear that he had called to speak with me. He asked me how I was doing, expecting that I would have done the surgery already and was now recovering or recovered and back at work. He greeted me by stating he hoped I was doing much better. I responded frankly by telling him I was doing much worse. With a deepened sigh, he went on to ask what was the matter. I related how my surgery was still not done and how disheartening and overwhelming it was. He went on to share a similar situation he had been in and how it was the intervention of his sons that helped him not lose sight of the same tardiness in the medical system. He understood my pain as he empathized with me, then he asked me to bow my head as he prayed for me. I felt such warmth like a Father who came to the aid of his daughter just in time.

After praying, he decided to reach out to someone on my behalf. It turned out that the person he contacted was of a very high caliber and had the right connections to get things done.

GOD'S EXPLICIT RESPONSE

Although the song "Trust in You" by Lauren Daigle was one of my favorites—I have listened to it a lot of times—something special jumped out at me as it played in the background while I wrote my story. Often, we listen to songs and fall in love with them, but it takes a deep situation where each word plays out explicitly to send that intentional message to your soul. *Letting go of every single dream, I lay each one down at your feet;* it was as if the Holy Spirit visited me to show me what God really wanted from me. I needed to let go and literally let God. Even though I was saying it and trusting Him, I was looking for a certain response. I needed to really say, "*When You do not move the mountains I needed You to move or part the waters I wished I could have gone through or give the answers as I cry out to You, Lord, I will still trust in You.*" When we ask God to have His way, do we really mean it? Or in the back of our minds, we already figured out the way we want God to go? *Omnipotent, omniscient God, please forgive me and have Your way! Amen.*

Have you ever felt like you just wanted to gush out all that is within you to God? Like you just need a quiet place to cry out and tell Him everything you are feeling? This is what I felt, but I didn't find the right time and space.

Wednesday came, and I made up my mind to attend church for evening prayer, since we were on a one-month fast. After discussing testimonies of past miracles that God had performed, we began to pray. I began to pray, and there it was. The desire to pray with every fiber in me was there again, and I prayed like never before. I bawled; I asked God some serious questions, and I even challenged Him. I was very expressive and emotional. Ultimately, I felt empowered and at ease. It felt like all the weight had been rolled off my shoulders. Then He gave me a word through my pastor, *"If we endure, we will also reign with him. If we disown him, he will also disown us; if we are faithless, he remains faithful, for he cannot disown himself."* (2 Timothy 2:12-13 - NIV). I held on to this word, and it encouraged me.

After this, she asked seven people to lay hands on me and pray. When all hands were on my head, it felt like three bags of cement on my head pressing my neck into my shoulder. As I was about to ease them off, the voice of the Lord said to me, *"This is the weight of the anointing that I will place on you."* Then, immediately, He brought me back to something that happened approximately ten years ago. I was at a parish event where my church was asked to lead the worship session. As a new member of the team, I was there, but my experience was quite limited. I recall that the person leading was very anointed, and the entire building was on fire with the Holy Ghost. As I watched the manifestation of the Holy Spirit, I whispered, *"God, I would love for You to anoint me like that."* He then asked, *"Are you willing to pay the price?"* I replied, *"Yes."* When this clip played out in my mind, I was lost for words; it literally left me in awe. I wondered to myself, *"Who really are You, God? We really cannot fathom You."*

My next clinic appointment came, and I was hopeful. I was prayed up and felt like it was a day that nothing could go wrong. While I sat waiting to be seen by the doctor, I received some information. I would now receive only half of my monthly salary. I would need to write an extensive report to apply for additional time off from work and appeal for it to be granted with pay. I sat there and received the information with a smile. I then reassured myself that it was well. At the end of the visit, it seemed like I had another few appointments before I would be cleared for surgery. There was still no sign of the medical report needed to apply for financial assistance, so I could only wait.

The next day, I realized that my account had been hacked, and of the five hundred and forty-six thousand dollars saved towards my treatment, five hundred thousand was gone. I wondered if it was a prank; I could not understand. I had to sigh repeatedly.

I spent most of that day encouraging one of my church youths who was struggling, lost, and backslidden. I had not seen her for a long time, but was burdened for her in prayer to the point where I had to reach out and find her. As I encouraged her, I shared several testimonies of how trusting God was worth it, but the enemy was asking, *"Are you still sure that all you said today is true?"* However, I was led to revisit a video by Bishop T.D. Jakes entitled, "Steady in the Storm," and I was encouraged. He mentioned that an uncanny anointing deserved an uncanny storm, as God allows the storm to give you an experience that no one else was allowed to have in all their lives, so that you would know Him in a way that other people would not know Him. This was definitely an uncanny storm.

I decided to book an appointment with a top orthopedic doctor in the country. He was also the only doctor on the island who had initiated stem cell therapy and conducted several research studies and trials in this area of treatment, including those for avascular necrosis. This was now my final attempt to try and get the surgery done privately or to get a final opinion. What I did not know was that the lessons God was teaching me were not yet complete. I attended this appointment with an open mind, as I was only seeking God's perfect will at that point. I prayed and also asked some sisters to join me in prayer during the meeting.

My visit with this doctor was conclusive. It was evident that he was very knowledgeable in his field and was also quite honest. He assured me that the right hip definitely needed a joint replacement, the left shoulder could benefit from stem cell treatment, and he could see that the left hip was showing some indication of developing the same complication sometime in the future, so he would also recommend stem cells for it. However, with all that being said, he advised that, due to my medical history, he would recommend that I wait to undergo surgery at UHWI, as they have a full team to cater to all medical emergencies should any occur. He also paid close attention to the proposed treatment plan given to me by the Indian doctors and said he agreed that it would have been the very best option for my condition and that he would write the letter required. Although I was unsure his letter would be accepted since he was a private doctor, I still hoped to take it in—trusting God. After I left his office, this song took over my heart: *"After you have done all you can, you just stand."* I went into the car, looked for the song on YouTube, and as I played it, I just cried. I had literally done all I could and was still nowhere closer than where I started. All I could do now was just stand.

TESTIMONIES THAT BREAK CHAINS

It is important that when we go through storms, we learn to listen to what the Lord will impress upon our hearts because He is always teaching us something. Over that weekend, the Lord began opening my eyes as He spoke to me. He showed me that my temperament was that I always wanted to be in control of my situation; I had the earnest need of always wanting to know what is next, and even though I was saying I trusted Him, I only trusted to a point because I always had things figured out in my head. This was hard for me to learn, but I needed to understand that God expected total letting go and for me not to try to control anything, because He already had total control. I needed to believe that.

As I continued fasting for the second week of the twenty-one days, the Holy Spirit said to me, *"You will minister on Youth Sunday."* I took a breath as I thought of the fact that I could not stand but for even a very short time, and I was, most times, in pain from sitting up; however, I did not say anything. A few days later, the same voice spoke again, and this time I responded, *"Lord, if You give me a word, then I will do it."* Days passed, but I did not get a word.

Saturday came and, usually, our pastor would call if she was led for you to bring the Word. I was content because I did not receive that call, but later that afternoon, the call came, and even then, I did not receive a word. I was doing midnight prayers, so that night I was up at midnight, praying, seeking a word from the Lord, and reading, but no word came. I remember saying, *"God, I do not want a word that will speak about what I am going through. I want a word that will speak to Your people."* I went to bed, and I was awoken at 6 am with the words, *"Nothing about your life is wasted."* As I jumped up, I said, *"But God, that sounds like You are referring to me right now,"* and He responded to my heart,

"You cannot take people where you have never been." And just like that, He started downloading, and I started writing.

Romans 8:28, *"And we know that all things work together for good to them that love God, to them who are the called according to his purpose."* (KJV).

God works for the purpose of those who love Him and those who are called. If you love Him, you will experience His call and vice versa. Therefore, we need to understand that we are called and submit to His purpose so that all things, even when it is not for our comfort, will work for our eternal good.

Although nothing physically changed that week, a lot spiritually changed, and it was wonderful. The greatest change one can aspire to experience while going through a storm is a change in perspective. My perspective had continued to change for the better as I embraced the peace of God. As I took hold of the reality that God was in control, that He was preparing me for a prepared place, that my circumstances will not determine my destiny, I received a peace that was second to none. It is important to note that peace does not take away the storm; it does not stop the storm from escalating, but it sure does give tranquility in the midst of turmoil. I was literally at a place of, *"Let go and let God."* I had no idea what the next step with my job, scammed money, treatment, or appointments would be, but I was at peace. All I cared to do at that moment was to "stand."

Chapter 7

The Threshing

At the beginning of this journey, if anyone had told me that I would still be in the same physical position months later, I would never have believed it. Yet here I was. It was now February, and I still had no idea what was happening, but the greatest thing was that I was at peace. I had not lost my hope, joy, or faith but, most of all, I had not lost my praise. I was still believing God for divine healing, and I was even more determined that I wanted it to be divine.

I asked God for a sign that He would heal me on the final Sunday of the fast. As far as I could see, I got no sign. I was a little disappointed, but I still knew God was sovereign, so I held on to my faith. That week, I was led to a video by Apostle Joshua Selman titled "Unlocking Destiny: Signs That You are the Chosen in Your Family." That title would lead one to think that it was designed to build your confidence and make you proud, but, on the contrary, it was designed to crush pride and ego, sending you to a place of consecration. It also unlocked reasons why some prayer requests were not answered for us. He makes us aware of the different spirits we must fight as we encounter certain levels in our lives as children of God. I could not help but wonder, *"What would be my encounter if I had a testimony of divine healing from this situation?"*

Knowing my God is sovereign and that His wisdom is unsearchable, I held on to His Word. One day, while on the prayer line for midday prayer, I listened to Sis. Moveen (the leader of the Prayer line) as she went into deep praying and seeking God for a word for that day. As she presented the word and I listened, the Holy Spirit revealed to me that I was not just sick, experiencing delays to my healing, being attacked by enemies, going through a storm, left alone, but I was on the threshing floor.

"His winnowing fork is in his hand, and he will clear his threshing floor, gathering his wheat into the barn and burning up the chaff with unquenchable fire." (Matthew 3:12 – NIV).

The threshing floor was a place used by farmers. It was an outdoor space where farmers would spread the grain out over a stone or hard-packed dirt. Then, an animal, such as an ox, donkey, or horse, would walk across the grain to break the kernels. The outside shell of the grain would then need to be separated from the good part of the grain.

This is where the farmer would use the natural wind to help separate the grain from what was called **"chaff**." The word "chaff" means "rubbish." This was just the other parts of the grain that would not be used. The farmer would use a **"winnowing fork"** to throw up the chaff and the grain that was mixed together. The wind would blow away the chaff, and the heavy grains would fall back onto the threshing floor. The process was then repeated until all the rubbish had been removed and only the grain was left.

Like grain that was separated from the kernel, so was I being separated and processed to remove every chaff and to reform me into the image and likeness of God. It was during this time that God led me to a video, which brought me to tears, as it revealed that healing me was easy and part of the Master's plan for me. That would have been a good story for me to tell, while thousands more have that story to tell as well. However, only a few are trusted with a test you will not fail. If He does not heal me divinely as I hoped and I was still able to trust Him, testify of Him, serve Him, be faithful to Him, preach His word and, more importantly, manifest in the gift to heal others, then I would have a great story to tell and very few are able to tell that story.

Just as Sis. Moveen mentioned that it was impossible to be on the threshing floor and not learn anything, the Holy Spirit said, *"Take your diary and make a list of what you have learned in this season."* This was my list: Lessons learned on the threshing floor:

- **I have learnt total surrender** - being a person who always seek to have total control over my next move, my next plan, etc., I have learnt to give God every single detail of my life and to trust Him in all my battles, knowing that He has total control and I do not have to lean on my own understanding.

- **Separation to God alone.** I have always aspired to spend more time with God and experience that deep level of separation to Him, but was always so anxious and busy. I have experienced this and am still growing in it.

- I learned to remember God's promises and to hold on to them, even when everything else indicates otherwise.

- **Pursued God's plan always.** Many times, we are not mindful that things that go against our will and comfort may just be God's divine plan. But I have learnt that God sees everything ahead of time, and His plan is for my good, even when it is not for my comfort.

- **Be slow to speak.** Instead, spend time observing, discerning, seeking God, and waiting.

- **Pray always.** Stay in prayer and pray about everything. God does not act until men pray.

- **My reputation is not important; God's glory is.** So even if I am limping, I will always move forward.

- **Rest in God.** As long as I have committed something to Him, I can totally rest assured that He is working it out.

These lessons did not come easily. It took the removal of chaff, much threshing, many tears, and much waiting. It was a process of dying to myself, and I am still learning. Even as I write this book, I am still waiting, trusting, and seeking, but my perspective is quite different, and that is of utmost importance.

Chapter 8

When Pain Meets Prophecy

On February 21, I woke up early, had a prayer, and then went back to bed. I woke up at different intervals to read my Bible and watch some motivational videos. At one interval, I decided to check my account to see if my salary was paid. To my surprise, it was paid, but I was only paid half. Instantly, I began to smile when I saw how much my salary had been reduced, and I also remembered how excessive some of my bills had been, especially for that month. I laughed and said, *"Okay, God, here we go. It is well."* That was the word in church on Sunday.

I finally decided to get out of bed and go to the bathroom with my devotional. I read the chapter for the day, "Today is Your Best Day Because of Salvation" by Roy Lessin (2018). Instantly, I was reminded of an incident that happened twelve years ago. I was pregnant with my second child and at church on a Sunday when a word of knowledge was given by a minister. She repeatedly echoed, *"I was wounded and broken for you; nothing is impossible with Me."* She called several names and echoed the word to them. Even though she did not call my name, I heard the Holy Spirit say to me, *"Take out your diary and write down that word."* I hesitated, saying, *"It is not my word because she did not call my name."* Again, I heard Him say to me, *"Write down that word for the sake of assurance."* I wrote down the word, still thinking it was not really mine.

The next day was my first appointment to see a consultant at a popular hospital at their high-risk clinic regarding my pregnancy. He asked if it was my first pregnancy and if my first delivery had been normal. After responding to him that it was my second pregnancy and the first was delivered at that same hospital through normal delivery and the baby was doing well, he proceeded to tell me that I should go to another hospital which was more advanced and had better facility to cater for my case since I had sickle cell. I explained to him that, due to my job situation and the fact that I didn't have a ride, the next hospital would be too far, and regular visits would result in regular absences from my job, which I couldn't afford at the time. He meanly asked if I preferred my job over my life. I told him I was going to trust God to take me through, and he mockingly responded, *"You and that God thing huh."*

I was so distraught leaving that doctor's office that I could not stop crying. Nothing could comfort me until the Holy Spirit said, *"Take out your diary and look back at the word from yesterday."* It read even more meaningful this time, *"I was wounded and broken for you; nothing is impossible with Me."* It was then and there that I found comfort, hope, and peace like never before.

I sat in my bathroom and read the words from my devotional, *"Salvation means I sent my son to earth to die for you, be buried for you, and rise from the dead for you."* It was then that this memory of over twelve years came back to me and I was led to understand that at that time I was diagnosed with sickle cell disease, which was a threat to my pregnancy; now I was diagnosed with avascular necrosis, which is a threat to my healing. Here I was, another time, dealing with another consultant who wanted to block my way of deliverance because he saw the diagnosis, but he did not see the God behind the diagnosis. Yet I knew the God who was behind the diagnosis, so I did not back down, because I knew nothing would *be impossible for my God.*

I had barely finished the afternoon when I received a message from a friend who was a pastor. She said she heard about my condition and reached out to me to speak with someone she knew who had a child with a similar situation. I hesitated, but I went on the call that day with prayerful resolve. I was introduced to a product I had taken before, but after a while, it became too expensive and inaccessible for me, so I stopped taking it. Through conversation, I was reintroduced to health products that offered numerous benefits for my condition. Although I had no money and my condition seemed urgent, this person, out of generosity, sent me over twenty-five thousand dollars' worth of products that

I could start taking without even a down payment. This was God making a new way for me, and I was willing and ready to walk into this open door.

Since all the leave I had available had expired and I was unable to undergo surgery, I was required to go to work to secure my job. Expecting to return to work in a few days, I was feeling scared; I kept thinking about it, especially since every time I dreamed of returning to work, the dream was never a good one. It was in worship that the Lord gave me the assurance that I needed not to fear because He goes before me and is my defender behind me. I also remembered one day, as I asked for prayer for this request on the prayer line, the Holy Spirit spoke through one of His servants to assure me that He had created an open door, and I should walk in it. He also told me and confirmed that there was going to be an abundance of rain. One thing I learned to do was to always embrace and hold on to the spoken Word of God, and more and more, I was being tested.

I returned to work that Thursday, and it was a pleasant trip. His Word, as found in Psalm 23, was my comfort and guide in my return. The Word gave me such confidence that I was able to focus on something other than the pain. It was remarkable how my limping became less important, and I was able to push through using my cane without fear.

The favour of God was also very evident from start to end. Unable to sit too low without extreme pain, my principal instantly purchased a chair specially designed for me, along with other accessories to make me more comfortable. I was deeply grateful.

The days went by, but of course, the enemy could not resist the urge to show up. However, one of the most important things that emerged from all of this was the mantle my husband learned to take up as he prayed and anointed me every morning before he left the house. This allowed me to bear the kingly anointing that God required, as my husband is my covering. This was a very big answer to my prayers.

The days went by, and I was still praying, still logging on to the God prayer line as often as I could, and still doing my midnight prayers. On Tuesday, March 5, 2024, I was up at midnight, praying as I had every night since December. My sister-in-law was on the call with me, since we would sometimes pray together. After praying for over two hours in warfare, intercession, and petition, the Holy Spirit told me to sit still for three minutes. I was sort of concerned about the specification of the time; however, I did. When it got to the second minute, I heard, *"You are under an open heaven,"* and I saw a vision of the sky covered with gray clouds. Suddenly, an opening formed in the middle, shaped like a circle, and I was looking straight into the blue. I was so broken, I could hardly speak to explain to my sister-in-law what was happening. I then googled the meaning of "open heaven" and this is what I found: *"When the heavens are opened, God becomes real. The revelation of God, His kingdom, and eternal realities are released in powerful ways on earth. We go from the concept of God to the reality of*

God. From the omnipresence of God to the manifest presence of God. There are outpourings of the Holy Spirit, a harvest of souls, powerful miracles, healing, and deliverance. God's blessings are poured out, and His righteous judgments are released. Barriers in the spiritual realm are removed, and the veil between heaven and earth is torn. There is access on earth to the riches stored in heaven."[1]

It was an enriching experience, and I was yet to discover more. I ended the call and went to the bathroom; this was usually a place where God spoke to me expressly. As I sat there, I heard, *"There are some experiences you will not get until you pray them into existence. There are strategic prayers to lead you into different realms of the Spirit. This is why the Bible says, 'Men ought always to pray and not faint.' (see Luke 18:1). As you pray and make prayer your habit, your intimacy with God increases and the Holy Spirit, through the Word of God and the people of God, will lead you into praying certain prayers that will open all doors and the realms of heaven to you"* (see Acts 16:25).

This was mind-blowing. I retrieved my phone and began taking notes on my notepad. This was real! I was on the verge of moving to the next level of empowerment; I could feel it. Something superb was about to unravel, and all I had to do was wait for it.

---

[1] Excerpt from the online article: What is An Open Heaven? By Jake Kail Ministries, September 13, 2022

I didn't need to wait for long. The next day, I went to work, and it was business as usual, until I began to feel restless. I felt like I had to go home. I called for my ride and headed home, following my instinct at the time. As soon as I entered the house, I got a call. It was from the bank to inform me that they have reconsidered and will refund the money that was scammed from my account, which they had previously stated they would not refund, due to good customer relations. This was a miracle from an open heaven experience.

It was coming down to my next appointment for the clinic, and I was expected to be admitted for a week before the actual day of surgery. That same week was going to be an empowerment at church, and if all went according to plan, I would only be there for one night. I went to the appointment and was sent back home to return Monday for admission, which was perfect timing for me to attend all the empowerment nights, then return to the hospital. The empowerment was a heavenly experience; it felt like it was planned just for me. All the scriptures and word that God had been giving me secretly was opened by the speaker. There were so many confirmations to my spirit; I was overjoyed.

Monday came, and it was time for my admission. I went to the hospital and, as expected, the enemy had to show up, trying to frustrate the process, but the Holy Spirit helped me to keep calm with the help of the blood of Jesus throughout the day. In the end, I was admitted, testing started, and instead of being on a communal ward, I was given a private room and bathroom, which was just excellent for that moment.

I have come to understand that there is a grace called favour, and when it comes upon you, every man who looks at you will be appointed to favor you. It was also revealed to my spirit that even when you are under an open heaven, you will still have to fight for your miracle to manifest because the enemy does not give up or take breaks, and neither should we.

I had not thought about this revelation for long when I woke up to the reality of my very words. Here I was on the morning of my surgery, March 20, 2024. I woke up at 4:55 am and started preparing, only to be told that the company that was to deliver the implant would not be honoring the letter because of one word that was wrongly stated in the letter. Therefore, the procedure could not be performed at 8 am, and one doctor was quick to point out that it was now impossible to take place again that day. In an instant, I sensed the enemy working. There comes a point when you must know what God is saying to you and know when the enemy is creating a hindrance. I calmly turned my focus to another doctor on the team and asked, *"Since there were other surgeries for the day, could I be rescheduled with another?"* He humbly explained that due to the nature of my surgery, they usually do those first; however, there were two similar cases for that day before they moved to trauma cases, so if I were able to be ready for the second slot that was for about 10 am, then I would be next. I smiled and told him that was all I needed.

The reason I could do this was because I woke up to the memory of God being my *"I Am,"* which was one of the messages from the recent empowerment. He is all I need Him to be; He is All in All. When the first doctor stated it was impossible, my spirit responded that this is where God enters—in the impossibility. God had me make a few calls. I didn't even know I would have those kinds of contacts, but then again, when favour locates you, it is a divine encounter. I was still not perturbed because I knew God was in my story, and He had already paid for the outcome of the day. This is when my trust in Him manifested.

It was not weird that the very moment I woke up that morning, I felt in my spirit that I needed a word. After freshening up, I took out my favourite devotional, "Because of Jesus, Today is Your Best Day," and started turning the pages. I was not about to read from where I had read last time, but I was following His lead. These words caught my eyes, *"God has done everything for you and will be everything to you" (see Psalm 116:12).* I continued reading and there were a list of similar scriptures—very encouraging—so I turned to the front of the chapter and this is what it read: *"Today is Your Best Day Because God is Your All."* The scripture for the title read, *"Now when all things are made subject to Him, then the Son Himself will also be subject to Him who put all things under Him, that God may be All in All." (1 Corinthians 15:28 - NKJV).* My spirit yelled "Hallelujah" from my bones. This was so intentional. God has all things structured, and He speaks to us in many ways. I was just watching things work out for my good.

Immediately at 10:30 am, my brother was on location with the corrected version of the letter for the company to send off the implant. Little did I know that God was way ahead of me. I reached out to the manager to let him know my brother was now on location, and he said to me, *"Mrs. Warren, everything is in place for your surgery already. The devices are on location, and I also sent a confirmation to the head surgeon. Have a safe surgery."* And with that, He had just confirmed that He specialized in things that seemed impossible; Only He can.

That evening, after surgery, I was taken back to the ward. My family was there to help me settle in again. After they left, I took my phone to check my messages. There was a message from NCB saying, *'Congratulations, my money has been reimbursed to my account.'* I smiled and gave thanks to God. At that point, I was unaware that I had not received a salary for that month, but God was ahead of me yet again and had made provision for all my needs. It was then I confirmed His Word to me months before from Deuteronomy 28:12, *"The Lord will open the heavens, the storehouse of his bounty, to send rain on your land in season and to bless all the work of your hands. You will lend to many nations but will borrow from none." (NIV).*

I was discharged five days later from the hospital and started therapy at home that very week (which was seven thousand dollars per session), with a health card that had zero balance and medications that roughly cost a total of sixty-five thousand per month, and not knowing how I would afford any of it.

I had been confessing that I was travelling with my family that year, as it was one of my greatest dreams, and that led to the purchase of tickets from the reimbursed funds. I still wanted to pursue the treatment in India, and I still had not seen how it would work out, but I was trusting God. I believed it was my winning season; therefore, everything associated with me wins.

I was still on the prayer line and God gave a direct instruction to His woman servant that, *"The glory of the Lord has come. It would be a domino effect beginning with me."* We were informed that on April 12, 2024, a special service would be held on the prayer line, allowing us to experience the glory of God. This was a season of expectancy as we prayed, fasted, and prepared. It was my winning season. God had started it, and I was about to stay on board for the full course of the ride.

For the season leading up to the special service, we would meet every day via WhatsApp group call to pray regarding the meeting and declare the Word of the Lord. The day finally came, and I was one of the persons to share my testimony of how the Word of the Lord came about to construct the theme, *"The Glory of the Lord Has Come."*

It was true that things were turning around for me, but as is evidenced in this book, it did not start here. I testified of how God revealed Himself to me in an open vision one night after praying the midnight prayer. I testified of being on the threshing floor for so long and how God had removed the chaff of my life and had intentionally drawn me closer to Him. I experienced more peace, joy, and contentment, and I was also seeing the results of my prayers being answered. My money that was scammed was reimbursed by the bank, even though they said they would not reimburse it. My family was more together, my children were happier, I was seeing several evidence of the goodness of the Lord; my season was changing. From this point forward, I entered a different season. I could literally feel God's presence every time throughout the day, and I could ask Him for anything. My new song for the season was *"Hold it Together"* by Maverick City; this was my new declaration. He was still writing my story; He held it all together.

STILL STANDING, STILL PRAISING

I was still in a season of recovering all. I was going to be home for approximately six weeks to recover before I could return to work or church. By week three, I went for a post-op visit, and my bandage was removed. I was experiencing terrible nerve pain in the surgical leg, which was almost blinding, but I was taking painkillers for it. By the fourth week, I was taking a break from all pain medications and was back on my pain management. In week five, I tried driving again. By week six, I was able to hop around the house, and by week seven, I no longer needed a walker and only used a cane when outdoors.

During this time, my husband was able to travel to America for the first time, while the children and I stayed home. I was currently in week seven, looking forward to returning to church and to work, but I was no longer the girl I used to be. I had gone through an uncanny storm and came out with an uncanny anointing. I was never going back to where I was; I was never going to allow the enemy to get away with crossing my path again.

I was still believing God for the money to pursue the treatment from India, especially for my shoulder, which was still in so much pain. I was trusting Him for the way out.

On the first day of May, I received a call from an organization pledging a contribution of one thousand US dollars towards the treatment. Another organization gave thirty thousand, and by May 6, I was able to reapply for the letter from the consultant in order to apply for financial aid. Although I was not hearing from the doctor in India much, I knew God was still on the case. I had learnt how to lean and depend on Him. I had learned how to trust Him to make the way, and I had learned how to allow Him to be in control, listening for when He says to act and do just what He says to do. That was exactly where I wanted to remain. The season was passing very quickly, and as it was almost the end of the school year, I became very busy with work. However, I vowed to myself that busyness would never let me lose my spiritual focus again. Although I wasn't doing midnight prayers every night, I was committed to my various prayer times and family Bible study.

At one point, I started having second thoughts about the treatment in India, especially since I was still not near the financial target, and I had still not received the letter from the consultant. I started to question God about His will, and I was tempted to become flustered over the situation. One day in June, I received a call from the hospital to say the letter was ready. I took the day off work and went to pick it up, only to discover it was not signed, and all attempts to contact the doctor to sign it were futile. One would think it was the perfect opportunity to get really upset and quarrel, but instead I sat in my car and just said, *"Lord, I know You are saying something in all of this."* It was then revealed to me that I had to take that day because I also used the opportunity to take my brother to the clinic, and discovered he was really sick; it was a good thing he came. This was another situation that reminded me that, *"And we know that in all things God works for the good of those who love him, who have been called according to his purpose." (Romans 8:28 – NIV).*

I was not perturbed because I knew God still had a plan, so I kept praying earnestly for God to reveal His perfect will. I was determined that if this treatment was not God's will on my behalf, then I did not want it. I was intrigued at first by an organization that reached out willingly to help, even though it was a small one. They made a financial contribution to my account, and they encouraged me to start a GoFundMe page. Through that platform, I started receiving other contributions. Nevertheless, I was still praying, *"Lord, let only Your will be done."*

I completed the term at work, and by the end of it, I was walking without any aid, climbing stairs, and moving around quite comfortably. I was a miracle in plain sight; I was so grateful for God's goodness towards me.

It came down to the moment I had been looking forward to: the day to travel to the United States for the summer holiday. The greatest part was that I was taking my two children with me for the first time; this was a long-awaited prayer answered.

Two days before our flight, we came under a hurricane threat, and the flight was cancelled with the opportunity to rebook for another day. This was disappointing for the children, but I had a peace I could not explain. The hurricane actually arrived, and our house leaked badly; we were without electricity, water, and internet for days. It was remarkable how, in the midst of that, God would have it that I bonded with my children to a much greater degree during this time, as I encouraged them to see God's hand in the situation. We played games, we talked, and even camped out in our living room together.

The day to travel finally came. I was going back to my sister-in-law, who had previously taken care of me during my illness; my husband was there, and I was taking my two children. This was a supernatural blessing I could never explain. We enjoyed every moment of our travelling, mainly because our faithful Father sanctioned it.

One day, when I returned to Atlanta, I was outside playing with my nephew when my friend's husband, who was the one to escort me out of the hospital the previous year and had to manually take me up the stairs because I could not walk and could barely even stand, came by and saw me on the outside playing with my nephew. He stood and stared for a while, then he exclaimed, *"Nattalee! Look what the Lord has done! Oh my God!"* It was so amazing for him to see me moving around again, knowing my previous state. This almost brought him to tears. It was so great to see how the awesomeness of God puts us in awe.

One of the objectives of going to Atlanta that summer was to travel to India for the treatment. I was still not fully prepared and unsure of the outcome, but I was still holding on to hope. By this time, I could barely use my left arm, and any touch, no matter how slight, would send me into shocking, unbearable pain. Sometimes I would accidentally bounce on something or someone, and it would result in instant tears from my eyes and my whole body feeling like I was electrocuted. I was desperately in need of the treatment. I did not receive the letter of sponsorship from my government, so I would need to find 5,000 USD for treatment and an additional 500,000 JMD for airfare. With all the contributions I received, I was still not near my target, and I had done all I could at that point.

Donnie McClurkin asked in his song, *"What do you do when you have done all you can, and it seem it's never enough?"* He gave us the answer when he said, *"You just stand when there is nothing left to do, you just stand and watch the Lord see you through."*

There was nothing else to do but stand: stand on my faith, stand on all the words God gave me before, even though He was not speaking now. Stand on the promise I made to trust Him, even when it was hard. Stand on His promise that all things were working for my good; stand on my will to keep my praise—all I had to do was stand.

Was it easy? No! But was I going to quit? Absolutely not! Even though I had days when I cried, but never without hope, I had days when I sighed, when I could not pray the way I was accustomed to, and days when the burden got heavy and I felt overwhelmed. But despite it all, I was still standing.

WARRIOR IN WORSHIP

One morning in the early part of July, I woke up and felt overwhelmed. The GoFundMe account had not moved for days, and the situation seemed unlikely to change. I was texting a friend who was checking in on me and asked if I had reached the target for my treatment. My reply was, *"No, my love, I'm just trusting God with all my heart. I know so long as it's Daddy's will, He will work it out."* Of course, in the back of my head, the devil was whispering, but I intentionally let the truth overpower his voice. As I explained to her the grave pain I was in, she empathized with and encouraged me; that gave me another boost of faith.

Exactly one hour after that, I had to call her back to share my testimony with her. After our conversation, I told God that I knew He would work it out if it was His will. A little later, I received a call from an organization in Jamaica that I had written to several months before but had not received a response. I didn't even know I would be able to receive calls abroad, since my phone wasn't roaming. To my surprise, the lady on the phone informed me that they were calling in response to my letter and were contributing towards my treatment. The most supernatural part of it all was when she said the protocol was to send the money directly to the doctor, but because it was an overseas hospital, they would make an exception and send the money to my personal account. She wished me all the best and encouraged me to get well soon. Two days later, the contribution was in my account.

This may not have been hundreds of thousands of dollars, but I was abundantly grateful for every single contribution, and I was getting a confirmation of God's Word and will in all of them. I believe God was assuring me that He had my healing in His hand, and all I needed to do was continue to trust Him and wait quietly for Him (see Psalms 62:1). I was determined to do this. In addition, my aunt reached out to me that summer to find out how financially stable I was. When I told her of the struggles I was having, she decided to send some financial help. To my amusement, she also reached out to cousins, in-laws, and other family members, who started sending contributions as well.

One of the things I learned is that when you testify of God's goodness and declare your faith and gratefulness to the Lord, stand with your antenna raised high because you have disturbed the host of hell, the enemy will be waging war in revenge. Nevertheless, the devil has no new tricks, and he can never have the final say when your life is hidden in Christ.

Despite all these miracles that God was doing in my life, I would wake up some days and feel like the world was on my shoulders. Was it that I was not saved? Was it that I was ungrateful? I highly doubt it, but one thing was clear, I was able to relate to David when he cried out to God in many of the Psalms to save him again (see Psalm 69). I was able to relate to Paul, who said, *"For I do not do the good I want to do, but the evil I do not want to do—this I keep on doing." (Romans 7:19 - NIV).*

I could definitely relate to the children of Israel. Every time they came upon another challenge, they complained and forgot the God who had delivered them (see Exodus 16 and Numbers 11). However, I was assured that God's purpose in me must come to pass as Paul counseled us in 2 Corinthians 4:7-10, *"We now have this light shining in our hearts, but we ourselves are like fragile clay jars containing this great treasure. This makes it clear that our great power is from God, not from ourselves. We are pressed on every side by troubles, but we are not crushed. We are perplexed, but not driven to despair. We are hunted down, but never abandoned by God. We get knocked down, but we are not destroyed. Through suffering, our bodies continue to share in the death of Jesus so that the life of Jesus may also be seen in our bodies." (NLT).*

Regardless of what we face in life, God has already won the victory on our behalf.

It was my initial intention to travel to India during the summer holiday to receive the treatment for the condition I was facing. However, the visa took a while to be granted, and the ticket prices increased as the time drew closer. I soon had to weigh my options, and I decided to postpone my plans. During this time, I prayed and put my trust in God. However, as the Word highlights in the book of Numbers, the Israelites would follow the cloud that represented the presence of God and only move when the cloud moved. I was also watching the cloud. I remember someone declaring on the God's prayer line as we were meeting, *"At the right time, I, the Lord, will make it happen" (see Isaiah 60:22).* I wasn't sure if that Word was mine, but I received it and held on to it.

I had to return to work in September, so I decided to reschedule the trip for the end of September. I still didn't know how it would work, as it was still far-fetched, but God was still on the job. One thing about God is that when He is writing a story, He doesn't stop until it's completed. The most beautiful part of the events of this period was the peace that God had given me. I was not worried about what could happen or what could change because I was confident that God had it, and I was open to Him saying no at any point.

At the time when my patient care officer needed to apply for my brother's visa so that he could travel with me to India, he had some personal issues that caused delays. I was ignoring the urgency until the Spirit of God prompted me to reach out to him. I recall that it was one week before the application was finally submitted, and he told me to email them the day after to prompt a response. However, I did not feel the need in my spirit, so I did not. The following day, he told me again, so I decided to send an email.

A few days later, my brother forwarded an email to me stating that his visa had been denied. I was frightened, but I said quite calmly, *"Okay, God, I prayed for a sense of direction, so if this is You saying no, it is fine because I know whatever the outcome, You have it."* Though disappointed, I was not distraught. It seemed as if God was testing me. A few minutes later, my brother forwarded another email stating that his visa had been granted. I sighed and smiled. I just had to give God thanks for being so faithful. I started wondering if it had anything to do with the email I sent, and realized that the email had not been sent. I accidentally emailed myself; it had to be God on the case.

HEALED BUT NOT JUST FOR ME

Two mornings before my trip, I attended my church's prayer meeting on Zoom, which was a blessing as usual. At one point, my pastor, as she was praying, began to speak over my life. She said, *"The Lord is ensuring your healing. He is still working on your testimony. He has not brought you this far to leave you. He has a platform for you. You are going to be a minister. God healing you is not just for your job, but it is for His ministry because you will have to travel and share your testimony."* She said I should pursue the career God had instructed me to, because God had it planned. I received the word with a grateful heart.

Chapter 9

Warfare And Wellness

The time came for my trip back to Atlanta. Everything was falling into place, but that week, there was a whole lot of rain and threats of storms in Jamaica and Georgia, the very places I would be traveling to and from. The possibilities again looked daunting, to the extent that even school attendance was significantly affected, as students did not come in their usual numbers. But I remember saying to God, *"Lord, the winds and the rain must obey You, and it takes only a second for them to begin or end at Your command, so I will not worry about my flight."* The truth is that I had only planned to take two weeks off from work, and I needed things to work out within that timeframe. However, it was God who was in charge of time, and I was trusting His timing.

The day for my flight to Atlanta came, and the Lord had dried up all the rain. I had a long day before getting everything in place to travel and did not go to bed until a few minutes before 2:00 a.m., with the intention of waking up at

4:15 a.m. to get ready and be out by 5:00 a.m. I was so tired that my alarm went off, but unfortunately—or, I should say, fortunately—I fell right back asleep. It wasn't until 5:20 that my husband's alarm went off, waking me up. I was very late, and I had a stop to make, which was compulsory.

As if that was not enough, I called my brother, who was supposed to pick me up, and he said the keys were locked in the car. I got ready, and my husband reminded me that I had a spare key, which I hurried to find. Just before we drove out, I prayed, *"God, I put everything in Your hands today, and I thank You now, in Jesus' Name."* We went by my brother's, but the key had not been used for a while, so the batteries had died, and it was of no help.

As I watched my brother and my husband navigate around the car, trying to figure out what to do, I looked at the time and smiled, saying, *"Devil, I was looking for you to show up, but boy, you have some ways."* I began to rebuke him and said, *"It does not matter what you do, Satan, you cannot prevail because the blood of Jesus is already against you."* I started to pray, and in a few more seconds, the car door was open. I thanked God and smiled. We soon headed for the airport, and we were right on time because we were led by the God of time.

As I was checking in for my flight, I was in so much pain, and I was now having pain in my surgery leg as well as the opposite leg. This had just started, and I hadn't told anyone. The attendant asked if I was okay, and I told her yes, but she said I was not looking like I was okay. I smiled and told her I was feeling pain, but I would be okay. I finished checking in and was being pushed in a wheelchair. The truth is, I had not been okay for a long while. At that point, I was only living by faith, but that was enough to sustain me, especially when my faith was in the ultimate source. I was sure I would be okay; this was a fact.

I was a survivor reserved for God's plan. I was a survivor, poised to rebuild my land.

I arrived in Atlanta safely, and all was going well. I had three days before my flight to India, and I was to be accompanied by my brother. It is essential to note that the enemy does not relent in his schemes, so neither should we. We must maintain our vigilance and prayer. The Bible says, *"Watch and pray always." (see Luke 21:36).*

Two days before our flight, my brother became very sick. His temperature was 102 degrees, and he was in pain all over his body. I was tempted to worry, but then I was looking for the enemy; it's just that you never know where he will show up. I told my pastor that my brother was not doing well, and she advised me on what home remedies I could give him. I didn't get the chance to give it to him that day, and by the next day, he was a lot worse. He was so sick that his wife decided to take him to urgent care. A resounding "no" came from my spirit; he was not going to the urgent care. I went ahead and prepared the remedy, prayed over it, and gave it to him along with whatever else the Lord directed me to do.

I anointed him with oil and prayed over him. Within about an hour, he started feeling better, and the fever subsided. However, it was constant prayer that won. That night, my pastor and prayer team came on Zoom and prayed for us. The day of the flight, he felt better, and we could travel.

Chapter 10

Miracles In The Mundane

The flight to India took off, and it was going to be a very long trip. We traveled for two days and did not arrive at the hospital in India until 4:30 am on Friday. On each flight, we didn't buy seats to sit together, but the Lord favored us, and we always got to sit together. God's presence carried us through the entire journey. It was a miracle in itself.

When we landed in Mumbai, we had a three-and-a-half-hour drive ahead of us to get to the hospital. I was very tired and was often dosing off during the ride. However, when it was about twenty to thirty minutes left to get to the destination, this thought came to me, *"What if the hospital is not what you are expecting? What if it is old and shattered?"* Almost instantly, the thought came to me: *"Jesus was born in a manger. He came from a lowly estate, so lowly that many did not receive Him as the Messiah because they thought He came too lowly."* As this revelation hit me, I said, *"Lord, I thank You."* When I actually arrived at the place, the room was sufficient for both of us to stay. The food was not what we were accustomed to, but we had snacks that we could manage.

On Saturday morning, I was awoken by a doctor who came to give me a walk-through of what my day would be like. I then had a consultation with my specialist, did some examination tests, and was scheduled to begin treatment the next day.

Because of the time difference, I was able to join the prayer line almost midnight that day, as it was 1 pm in the USA. I joined in prayer and praise, and even testified to the many blessings that God had been bringing into my life. Being in India was a great miracle, and one of the most beautiful parts of the story was that I had afforded all I needed to the point of not owing anyone any money. God is indeed a provider, sustainer, and promise-keeper. To Him is due all honour, glory, and praise!

I woke up early on the day of my treatment, had devotion, had a shower, and went back to bed. Sometime later, I was summoned to make the final payment and was then accompanied to the operating theater. I wasn't scared or nervous; I was just relaxed. As I lay there on the bed, the nurses worked to get everything in place. I watched them intently and even asked them to snap a picture of me. They were amused by how comfortable I was; they even teased me that I was a social media pop star.

The protocol that was explained to me was that I was not going to be put to sleep; instead, I would be given a spinal injection for the procedure on my hip and a kind of anesthesia block for my shoulder. I prayed about it, asking God for His will to be done. We were in the operating room for over an hour waiting for the anesthesiologist, who took a very long time to come. I was getting weary and flustered. However, when he came, he brought a presence with him—a presence of hope, comfort, and assurance. As he greeted me with a warm, friendly, and reassuring smile, he took my file and read a portion of it, reviewing some test results. It was then that he advised that he would be giving me general anesthesia. He asked if I had any concerns, and I replied that I did. I was concerned because of what my doctors in Jamaica had suggested and all the delays they put me through when I was to do my hip replacement, because they were afraid for my life due to the previous blood clots. He assured me that all would be well and I was getting just the right amount of sedation to last no longer than thirty minutes, and he was sure it was the best option for me. Still a bit traumatized from the whole ordeal of my previous surgery where I was wide awake, I was willing to go with this. After the whole procedure, I remember waking up to his voice as he said, *"Nattalee, wake up."* I was in so much pain; it was unbelievable. Right then and there, I was glad I had not been awake during the procedure. It was definitely the right choice for me.

When you pray and have people praying, this is how God will change protocols, legislatures, and procedures on your behalf.

There is no limit to what God will do for you.

The next day, I was restricted to bed until the afternoon when I was allowed to do my first session of physiotherapy. I literally could not walk, could not move my legs, and took at least three minutes just to sit up at the edge of my bed. The treatment was a lot more invasive than I had imagined. I started to wonder how I would manage to travel the next day to return to Atlanta and then be back in Jamaica for work on Monday. This was my schedule, and I needed to do all I could to make it work.

At the end of therapy that day, I was able to draw myself across the room. It was still an ordeal for me to use the bathroom independently, but I began to embrace the challenge.

The next morning, I was able to take a shower and get dressed. Although still in a lot of pain, I was walking a little better, and I wanted to travel that evening. I had a headache and was very weak and dizzy; I knew something was off. I requested another complete blood count to be done, as I knew my blood count was not within its normal range. I was indeed correct; my blood count had fallen, my monthly cycle came, and my legs and shoulder were in so much pain. Oh my gosh, it was a horrible day to be travelling.

It took us four and a half hours to get to the airport. Rain fell horrendously, accompanied by rounds of lightning so frightening that we wanted to run; thunder that sounded like God beating drums on the earth filled the air. My brother and I, with wide, popping eyes, stared at each other, speechless. After what felt like a week of checking in, we arrived at our gate, boarded the flight, and were finally on our way. I will never forget the relief I felt that moment as I sat down and realized that my seat was in the aisle, very close to one of the restrooms. This was ideal for my current status. I breathed a sigh of relief.

My relief was short-lived as a flight attendant approached me, asked for my name, and stated that my brother and I needed to accompany her off the plane because she had received a call indicating that something illegal was in my bag. I was lost for words, like *"What? Are you serious?"* I felt like a bomb was exploding on me. For a moment, I was speechless again, thinking this must be a mistake. However, as the moments passed, I recognized that they were quite serious, and we were indeed their targets. We were left with no choice but to collect all our luggage and disembark the plane. My brother protested, but to no avail. I really wanted to protest, but I was so weak and in pain that I just sat there feeling helpless, but not hopeless.

We were taken to a point and asked to sit and wait. We waited for hours before a security guard came to escort my brother to sort out the bags, while I waited. At one point, I cried as I thought about the fact that we were both good citizens. My brother is an army personnel in the US Forces, and I am an educator. Throughout our lives, we have served our country, and this was undeserving of us. However, I remember saying to him, *"Bro, let us not worry about this because I know that everything, even when it's ugly, happens for a purpose."* He nodded and said, *"That's true, sis."*

The morning ended with them figuring out that the item in the suitcase was only a keychain, which was actually a bottle opener in the shape of a bullet. This belonged to my brother, who liked such items because of his line of work, and he had been telling them this from the initial stage. In the end, they recognized that they were at fault, and we were hosted in a hotel room at the airport and booked for the next flight the following morning. Additionally, we were rewarded with a complimentary meal and a foot massage.

Was this a miracle? Oh yes, it was because I was so weak and sick that if I had taken that flight of nine hours, three hours layover, and another eight and a half hours to Atlanta, there is no telling what the outcome would be. The truth is, I needed more rest after such an invasive procedure before returning to a hectic schedule.

That day, I slept in that hotel bed like a baby. It was one of the best sleep I've ever had; it was so well-deserved. What was even more miraculous was that, without needing to provide much explanation, I was easily granted another five days of leave from work. I rested in Atlanta for a week before returning home at a cost of only twenty-five US dollars to change my flight date.

Chapter 11

Rewriting The Narrative

My week of rest was a reflection; I was still in awe after everything. I will never forget the revelations I had afterward.

Jeremiah 29:11 states, *"For I know the plans I have for you," declares the Lord, "plans to prosper you and not to harm you, plans to give you hope and a future." (NIV).* This was my devotional one morning; however, it was the first time I recognized what was said in the previous verse. This is what the Lord says: *"When seventy years are completed for Babylon, I will come to you and fulfill my good promise to bring you back to this place. For I know the plans I have for you," declares the* LORD, *"plans to prosper you and not to harm you, plans to give you hope and a future." (Jeremiah 29:10-11 – NIV).* The plans God has for us do not mean we will not face hardship, disappointments, and challenges. These people were in exile for seventy years, yet God still had a plan for them. His plan is always to redeem, rescue, preserve, and heal. All of this will take a process, but the end result is always for our benefit. I was moved to tears as this message resonated in my heart, and I realized, *"There is nothing that God will not do for me. He is the author of my story."*

The day to return home finally came, and I was excited about all God had done and was still doing. A few nights before, the Holy Spirit impressed on my heart to call a friend of mine whose daughter was a past student of my school. I knew she had written a book, and I was wondering what the process was for taking words on a laptop and turning them into a finished, edited, and published manual with a cover. I didn't think I was at that stage yet, but out of obedience, I made the call. To my surprise, the conversation went well over an hour, and it was ordained that I would make the call that night because I had a word in season to offer her, and she was the person God wanted me to connect with for the next step in the plan He had for me. I did not even have a proper name for my book yet, but I recalled that during our conversation, she asked what I had in mind. As I threw out the ideas of the titles I had in mind, she gave me a lasting suggestion.

It was on Saturday morning, however, the day of my return to Jamaica. I woke up at 6 am that morning, much earlier than the 10 am I had planned. The Lord led me, and I went back to retrieve the laptop I had already packed to update my story. Then and there, the full title was revealed to me. It was my reward for moving in obedience.

LEGACY OF A WARRIOR

I returned to Jamaica, and days later, I became very ill. God would have it that I attended a Youth Leaders empowerment, and my bishop called me out after he finished preaching and anointing. He then put on the jacket he wore while preaching on me and declared a covering of healing and restoration over me. Days after, I went into a terrible sickle cell crisis that lasted for about a week. During that time, it was the jacket given to me by my bishop that I slept in, and my pastor's prayer at my bedside that brought me through.

This total experience lasted for almost two years, but through it all, there was never a moment when God had not gone before me, stayed beside me, and covered me from behind. I came out of that situation in awe; I will never be the same. My worship was never the same. I do not think many people understood me hereafter, but I was different. I lost friends after this ordeal, and my circle changed without my input. However, I was in a much better place. I was transformed.

I finished that year on a very different note from where I started. The overwhelming, never-ending, reckless love of God had brought me so much grace; my testimony during that watch night service was such a powerful, overcoming victory. It was evident that God was not done with me, and the best part was that He was really just getting started.

The beautiful thing about restoration is that it occurs in every aspect of our lives simultaneously. It also results in God's will being accomplished and moves individuals away from emptiness to being truly fulfilled in God. Restoration gave me something important to talk about and provided me with a powerful story of transformation. I could not stop testifying, but all my testimonies were always such a little part of so much that had happened. It was then that I realized, from the beginning, when the Lord said, *"Start writing,"* that He was actually taking me on an unforgettable journey.

On March 20, 2025, when I celebrated the one-year anniversary of my hip surgery, I had to testify; I could not stop the tears from falling, as there was so much gratitude. In June, as we celebrated prize-giving at school, I led the devotional exercise, and tears were shed again. Many did not understand; they just thought I was too emotional, only I knew the number of my scars, and these were equal to the number of my victories.

I was promoted to supervisor of my grade while teaching a class of 32 students, plus preparing them for the Primary Exit Profile (PEP) exams; I was present every day with little or no pain. Witnessing 30 of them being awarded and seeing how God turned my story around was a glorious legacy. I could also see the ending of my favourite song when it said, *"Down through the years, I'd look on this moment and see God's hand on it and know He was there."* I can certainly say, *"Oh Oh Oh, my God did not fail."* So even if I had to be undignified and misunderstood in my praise, I had to let it out every chance I got. I had a story to tell.

One of the things I promised the Lord is that I would not refuse to share my testimony, declare His Word, and contend for the faith, developing a generation that will live beyond me.

Sickle cell is a diagnosis, but it is definitely not my destiny. We were born for a powerful purpose, and we can and should find that purpose through the eyes of the Spirit of God. I will indeed endeavour to walk in His purpose, fulfilling His will as He dictates the place and time. After all, He is not done with me!

References

1. What Does 'Threshing Floor' Mean for Christians Today?
   Sarah Frazer Crosswalk.com Contributing Writer updated October 2020

2. Because of Jesus Today is your best day, Roy Lessin - Senior Writer and Co founder of DAYSPRING 2018
   Jeremiah 29 NIV - A Letter to the Exiles - This is the - Bible Gateway - www.biblegateway.com - Saturday October 19, 2024

www.ingramcontent.com/pod-product-compliance
Lightning Source LLC
Chambersburg PA
CBHW060417090426
42734CB00011B/2344